THIRD YEA… ASSESSMENT PA…

REASONING

ANSWER BOOK

J M BOND

Nelson

Thomas Nelson and Sons Ltd
Nelson House Mayfield Road
Walton-on-Thames Surrey
KT12 5PL UK

51 York Place
Edinburgh EH1 3JD UK

Thomas Nelson (Hong Kong) Ltd
Toppan Building 10/F
22A Westlands Road
Quarry Bay Hong Kong

Distributed in Australia by

Thomas Nelson Australia
480 La Trobe Street
Melbourne Victoria 3000
and in Sydney, Brisbane, Adelaide and Perth

First published by Thomas Nelson and Sons Ltd 1966
Second edition 1983
Revised edition 1986

Pupil's Book ISBN 0-17-424473-8
NPN 9 8 7
Answer Book ISBN 0-17-424474-6
NPN 9 8 7

By the same author

Introductory, First, Second, Third and Fourth Year Assessment Papers in Mathematics

Introductory, First, Second, Third and Fourth Year Assessment Papers in English

First, Second and Fourth Year Assessment Papers in Reasoning

Filmset in Nelson Teaching Alphabet
by Mould Type Foundry Ltd
Leyland Preston England

Printed in England
by Ebenezer Baylis & Son Ltd
The Trinity Press Worcester and London

Paper 1

Underline the two drawings in each line which are exactly the same.

1–2
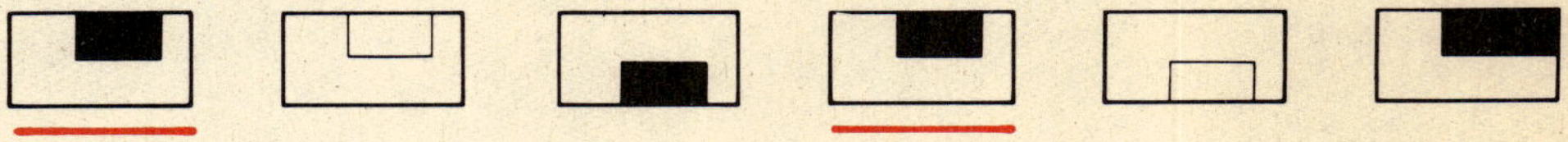

3–4
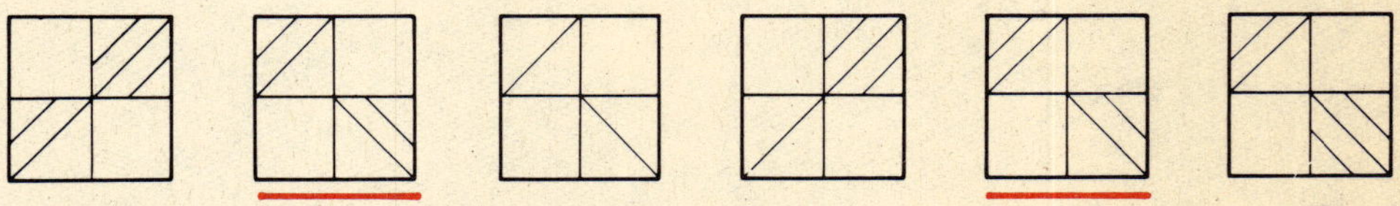

5–6
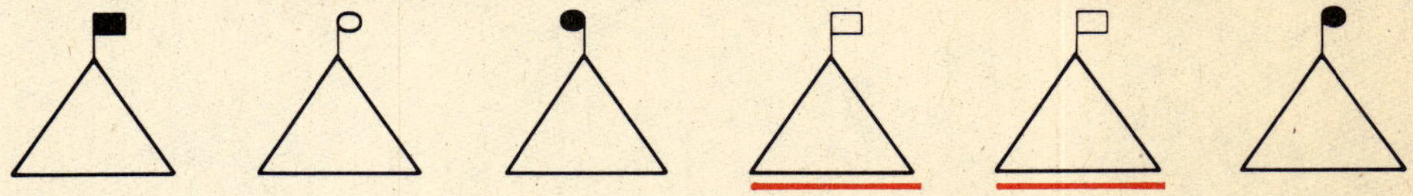

a b c d e f g h i j k l m n o p q r s t u v w x y z

7 If, in the alphabet, **y** comes before **p**, write **x**. If not, write **z**. ....z....

8 If there are four letters between **a** and **f**, write **o**. If there are more, write **m**. ....o....

9 Which day of the week starts with the 23rd letter of the alphabet? ....Wednesday....

10 Which month of the year starts with the 6th letter? ....February....

11 Lisa was born on 2nd January, 1973. Sally is two days older. When was Sally born? ....31st December, 1972....

12 Jennifer is shorter than George who is taller than Tom. Who is the tallest? ....George....

Fill in the space in each line by continuing the sequence.

13	a1	b2	c3	d4	e5	....f6....
14	ab	bc	cd	de	ef	....fg....
15	cg	ch	ci	cj	ck	....cl....
16	kb	lb	mb	nb	ob	....pb....
17	123	234	345	456	567	....678....

In a cricket match Michael scored four more runs than John who scored one run fewer than David. David made 23 runs.

18 How many runs did John score? ....22....

19 How many runs did Michael score? ....26....

This chart shows the attractions offered by five seaside hotels.

20–21 Which two hotels have the same attractions?
(Ocean Hotel, Beach Hotel, Golden Sands Hotel, Coral Reef Hotel, Bay Hotel)

22 Which hotel has children's activities, tennis and riding?
(Ocean Hotel, Beach Hotel, Golden Sands Hotel, Coral Reef Hotel, Bay Hotel)

23–24 Which two hotels do not have children's activities?
(Ocean Hotel, Beach Hotel, Golden Sands Hotel, Coral Reef Hotel, Bay Hotel)

25 Which hotel does not have water sports?
(Ocean Hotel, Beach Hotel, Golden Sands Hotel, Coral Reef Hotel, Bay Hotel)

Here are some words, and underneath are the words written in a number code. The numbers are not underneath the right words. Can you sort them out?

rink	kin	ink	rank
935	7159	7359	359

26 **rink** should be 7359

27 **rank** should be 7159

28 **ink** should be 359

29 **kin** should be 935

30 In this code, which of these numbers could stand for **near**?
3617 5717 5617

Underline the sum on each line which does not have the same answer as the sum in the left-hand column.

31	**(3 × 4) ÷ 6**	(5 × 4) − 10	(4 × 5) ÷ 10	(1 + 5) − 4
32	**(6 + 7) − 4**	(2 × 4) + 1	(3 × 3 × 1)	(2 × 5) + 1
33	**(5 + 4) − 3**	(5 × 1) + 1	(14 ÷ 7) × 2	(18 ÷ 3)
34	**(3 + 3 + 1)**	(21 ÷ 3)	(28 ÷ 7)	(3 × 3) − 2
35	**(4 × 2) − 7**	(7 − 6) × 0	(5 + 4) − 8	(6 ÷ 3) − 1

This chart shows the average day and night temperatures of three towns in three months of the year.

	June		July		August	
	day	night	day	night	day	night
Cairo	35°C	20°C	36°C	21°C	35°C	22°C
Cape Town	18°C	8°C	17°C	7°C	18°C	8°C
London	20°C	11°C	22°C	14°C	21°C	13°C

36 Which of these towns has the highest day time temperature? (Cairo, Cape Town, London)

37 In which month is this? (June, July, August)

38 Which has the lowest night time temperature? (Cairo, Cape Town, London)

39 In which month is this? (June, July, August)

40 Which town has the same night temperature in two months? (Cairo, Cape Town, London)

41 Which town has the biggest difference in its night time temperatures? (Cairo, Cape Town, London)

Five children did a test for which 100 marks were awarded. Rachel gained 96 marks. Mark had half as many marks as the person who came top. George lost five marks. Daniel had seven marks fewer than George, and Sarah had twelve marks fewer than Rachel.

42 Who was top? Rachel

43 Who was second? George

44 Who was third? Daniel

45 Who was fourth? Sarah

46 Who was bottom? Mark

Place the correct sign in the following spaces.

47 3 × 4 = 12

48–49 17 = 8 + 8 + 1

50 9 = 14 − 5

51–52 3 × 4 = 6 × 2

53 56 ÷ 8 = 7

54–55 3 + 17 = 21 − 1

Underline the correct answer in the brackets.

56 Are leaves always green? (Yes, no)

57 Is December always the last month of the year? (Yes, no)

58 Are there always twenty-eight days in February? (Yes, no)

59 Is Christmas Day always the coldest day of the year? (Yes, no)

60 Is a circle always round? (Yes, no)

61 I was born in 1966 and my sister is three years younger than I am so she was born in (1963, 1969, 1970, 1968).

62 I am 6 cm shorter than Jane who is 1·54 m so I am (1·44 m, 1·60 m, 1·48 m, 1·50 m) tall.

63 Mr. Brown is Alison's uncle so she is his (daughter, aunt, nephew, step-daughter, niece).

64 A cygnet is a young (goose, duckling, swan, hen, eagle).

65 As Graham was cycling to school he saw this road sign  so he knew he was coming to a (roundabout, level crossing, major road, crossroads, school).

Lorraine is shorter than Robin but not as short as Julie.

66 Who is the tallest? Robin .... 67 Who is the shortest? Julie ....

Underline one word in each line which does not fit in with the others.

68	cod	steak	haddock	plaice	sole
69	elm	oak	sycamore	rose	beech
70	England	Italy	France	Germany	Europe
71	rain	weather	snow	hail	frost
72	metre	millimetre	kilometre	litre	centimetre

Underline the correct answer in each line.

73–74 $\frac{1}{2}$ is to 1 as (3, 2, 4) is to (4, 5, 10)

75–76 $\frac{1}{4}$ is to 1 as (4, 2, 1) is to (12, 6, 4)

77–78 3 is to 9 as (4, 5, 6) is to (10, 12, 16)

79–80 Tuesday is to Wednesday as (May, March, April) is to (March, May, July)

81–82 Puppy is to dog as (cat, lamb, ewe) is to (dog, sheep, pig)

83–84 Author is to book as (man, sculptor, artist) is to (picture, paint, woman)

Paw is to dog as (puppy, leg, foot) is to (man, fish, cat)

87–88 Plate is to eat as (knife, cup, water) is to (drink, fork, saucer)

89–90 Aunt is to niece as (mother, uncle, nephew) is to (nephew, boy, sister)

91 If I had 12p more I should have twice as much as Jason who has 16p. How much have I? 20p

92 Kim is 14. Two years ago she was three times as old as John. Next year she will be three times as old as Andrew. How old is John now? 6 years

93 How old is Andrew now? 4 years

94 If I was 1 cm taller I would be 3 cm shorter than Bernard who is 1·49 m. How tall am I? 1·45 m

95 Samantha's birthday is on 28th February. My birthday is eleven days before Samantha's and Catherine's is four days after mine. When is Catherine's birthday? 21st February

Peter and Justin like cricket.
Paul and Stephen like football.
Peter and Paul like swimming.
Justin and Stephen like fishing.

96 Who likes cricket and swimming? Peter

97 Who likes fishing and cricket? Justin

98 Who likes football and fishing? Stephen

99 Who likes football and swimming? Paul

100 If 28th February 1968 was a Wednesday, 2nd March 1968 was a Saturday

Paper 2

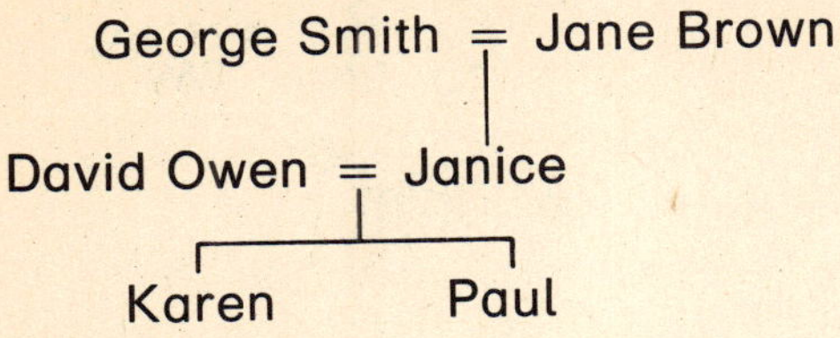

From this family tree find out the surnames of these people.

1 Karen ....Owen.... 2 Paul ....Owen....

3 Jane ....Smith.... 4 Janice ....Owen....

5 David ....Owen....

6 How many daughters had George Smith? ....1....

7 How many grandchildren had he? ....2....

Write the letter which occurs most often in the following words.

8 soap wash bath clean tap ....a....

9 If this letter is one of the first five letters of the alphabet, write **x**; if not, write **z**. ....x....

Which letter is found most often in the following words?

10 window room wood mirror wardrobe ....o....

11 If this letter is found after **p** in the alphabet, write **x**; if not, write **z**. ....z....

There are two things which tell you whether a number can be divided by 6:

(1) It must be an even number.

(2) The sum of the figures must be divisible by 3.

12–14 Underline any number which is divisible by 6.

197 <u>468</u> <u>354</u> 272 459 <u>156</u>

Complete the following sets.

15	pack	peck	16	ware	wart
	ball	bell		pare	part
	band	....bend....		mare	....mart....
17	sing	wing	18	hate	heat
	sink	wink		fowl	flow
	sail	....wail....		hire	....heir....
19	peal	pale	20	mile	lime
	bear	bare		sent	nest
	deal	....dale....		love	....vole....

Here are the names of some famous people, and the periods for which some Kings of England reigned.

William Wilberforce (helped to abolish slavery) born 1759
Duke of Wellington (beat Napoleon at Waterloo) born 1769
James Watt (designed first steam engine) born 1736
George Stephenson (built the "Rocket") born 1781
Napoleon Bonaparte (beaten by Wellington) born 1769

Kings of England

George I	1714–1727
George II	1727–1760
George III	1760–1820
George IV	1820–1830

21 Wilberforce was born in the reign of (George I, II, III, IV)
22 Wellington was born in the reign of (George I, II, III, IV)
23 Stephenson was born in the reign of (George I, II, III, IV)
24 Watt was born in the reign of (George I, II, III, IV)
25 Napoleon was born in the reign of (George I, II, III, IV)

Here is part of the contents list of a cookery book.

	Page
Puddings and sweets	17
Bread and scones	29
Pies and pastry	43
Biscuits	52
Cakes	61
Icings	72

On which page would I look to find the following recipes?

		Page
26	Jam tart	43
27	Malt loaf	29
28	Ginger snaps	52
29	Swiss roll	61
30	Butter icing	72
31	Chocolate pudding	17

Put the following words in alphabetical order.

court chest certain clothes captive

32 (1) captive   33 (2) certain
34 (3) chest   35 (4) clothes
36 (5) court

Some of the words below have been jumbled up. They are all connected with time. See if you can sort them out.

37–38 There are sixty **snodces** seconds in a **utmine** minute, and the
39–40 number of **thonsm** months in a **arye** year is twelve. There
41–43 are **neevs** seven days in a **kewe** week. **Stuuga** August
44 is the **thhgie** eighth month of the year.

45–47 Which of these numbers are divisible by 6?

1245 1326 1356 1760 3663 2334

Underline the largest in each line, and put a ring round the smallest.

48–49	month	week	minute	day	year	hour
50–51	723	372	273	327	732	237
52–53	chapter	word	paragraph	letter	book	sentence
54–55	343	534	543	345	535	353
56–57	some	none	all	most	few	more
58–59	1023	2301	1032	1203	2103	1302

Fill in the following spaces.

60	91	82	73	64	55	46	37
61	1·91	2·82	3·73	4·64	5·55	6·46	7·37
62	108	96	84	72	60	48	36
63	$\frac{1}{2}$	$\frac{3}{4}$	1	$1\frac{1}{4}$	$1\frac{1}{2}$	$1\frac{3}{4}$	2
64	70	63	56	49	42	35	28
65	66	77	88	99	110	121	132

In each line two of the drawings are different from the others. Underline those two.

66–67

68–69
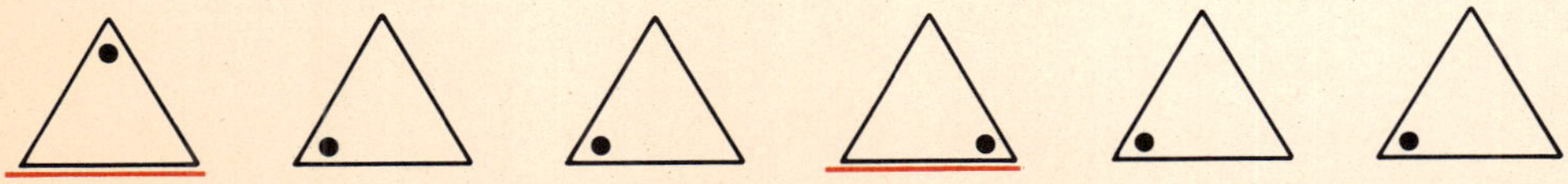

70–71

In the second group of words there is a word which has a similar meaning to a word in the first group. Underline both words.

72–73 pleased, praised, present — birthday, glad, song
74–75 council, comrade, console — enemy, combine, companion
76–77 alarm, against, adhere — stick, dock, war
78–79 permit, prevent, persuade — ask, allow, confess
80–81 ascend, obtain, abandon — descend, divide, leave

Answer the following questions by underlining the correct reply in the brackets.

82 Are there sixty months in five years? (Yes, no)
83 Has a triangle four sides? (Yes, no)
84 Are there twenty-four hours in a day? (Yes, no)
85 Are there twenty-four letters in the alphabet? (Yes, no)
86 Are mothers always older than their daughters? (Yes, no)
87 Is pork the meat we get from the calf? (Yes, no)

a 2 b 3 7 4 c b 1 8 7 d 5 y 3

88 Add all the even numbers in the list above. 14
89 Add all the odd numbers. 26
90 Which letter appears twice? b
91–92 Which numbers appear twice? 3 and 7
93–94 Write the numbers which come between two letters. 2 and 5

Add a letter to the word on the left to make another word with the given meaning.

95 **sight** slim slight
96 **fiend** a person one likes friend
97 **dead** to fear dread
98 **feet** a lot of ships fleet
99 **pose** the opposite of verse prose
100 **den** to say it's not true deny

Paper 3

a b c d e f g h i j k l m n o p q r s t u v w x y z

1 If the alphabet was written backwards, what would be the 5th letter? v

2 Which letter of the word **union** comes first in the alphabet? i

3 Which letter of the word **produce** is not found in the word **proceed**? ....u

4–6 Underline any of the following words which have their letters in alphabetical order.

hat beg man cot fly leg

7 Which letter of the alphabet is as far from **a** as **w** is from **z**? ....d

8 Which year is 10 years before 1904? (1914, 1804, 1894, 1903)

9 100 years after 1666 was (1766, 1676, 1667, 1665)

10 1 year after 1889 was (1880, 1890, 1789, 1879)

11 100 years before 1509 was (1499, 1609, 1489, 1409)

12 Which year was 100 years after 1601? (1591, 1691, 1701, 1501)

Here is part of a 1st Division Football League table.

	played	points
Ipswich	18	38
Manchester City	21	35
Manchester United	19	33
Southampton	19	33
Swansea	21	33
Nottingham Forest	19	32
Liverpool	18	30

13–14 Which two teams have played the most matches? (Ipswich, Manchester City, Manchester United, Swansea, Southampton)

15–16 Which two teams have played the fewest matches? (Ipswich, Liverpool, Nottingham Forest, Southampton, Manchester City)

17–18 Which two teams have played the same number of matches, and got the same number of points? (Ipswich, Liverpool, Manchester United, Nottingham Forest, Southampton)

Draw a circle round the figure in the second column which should logically fit in the space in the first column.

19

20

21

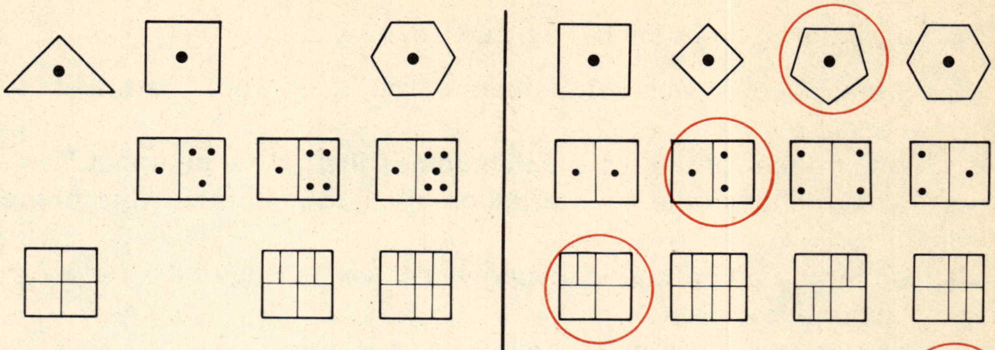

22 $\frac{a+b}{c}$ $\frac{c+d}{e}$ ___ $\frac{g+h}{i}$ | $\frac{d+e}{f}$ $\frac{h+i}{j}$ $\frac{a+b}{c}$ $\frac{e+f}{g}$

23 $\frac{876}{7}$ $\frac{765}{6}$ $\frac{654}{5}$ ___ | $\frac{876}{7}$ $\frac{543}{4}$ $\frac{765}{6}$ $\frac{987}{8}$

Underline two things in each of the following questions.

24–25 What does a bird always have? (Wings, cage, seed, feet)
26–27 What does a tree always have? (Roots, weeds, moss, branches)
28–29 What does a foot always have? (Hair, toes, sock, sole)
30–31 What does a car always have? (Engine, wheels, petrol, luggage)
32–33 What does a garden always have? (Soil, flowers, plants, grass)
34–35 What does a room always have? (Furniture, walls, floor, pictures)

There is a number, or amount, in each line below which does not fit in with the others. Underline it.

36	81	72	64	54	45	36
37	1	2	4	9	16	32
38	$1\frac{1}{2}$	3	$4\frac{1}{2}$	6	$8\frac{1}{2}$	9
39	107	105	106	104	105	104
40	46	42	38	34	32	26
41	2	10	3	11	4	8

In each line put a ring round the largest and underline the smallest.

42–43	city	country	village	continent	town
44–45	$\frac{1}{4}$ hour	20 minutes	one day	20 hours	$\frac{1}{2}$ hour
46–47	$10 \div 2$	$14 \div 7$	$16 \div 4$	$12 \div 2$	$15 \div 3$
48–49	1798	1965	1867	1743	1956
50–51	metre	centimetre	decimetre	millimetre	kilometre

52 If it is 11.25 a.m., how many more minutes will there be before it is noon? 35

53 If it will be Tuesday tomorrow, what day was it the day before yesterday? Saturday

54 Which day of the week has the largest number of letters in its name? Wednesday

55 In two years Paul will be twelve. Peter is three years younger than Paul. How old is Peter? 7 years

56 Margarine is cheaper than butter but dearer than lard. What is the cheapest? lard

57 Which of these years is a Leap Year? (1981, 1982, 1983, 1984, 1985)

Here are some sums. Look carefully at the signs to see what kind of sum they are. Fill in the missing figures.

58–59
```
   4 3
 + 2 8
 -----
   7 1
```

60–61
```
   7 9 0
 - 1 6 8
 -------
   6 2 2
```

62–63
```
   2 3 4
 ×     4
 -------
   9 3 6
```

64–65
```
     5 5
 3 ) 1 6 5
```

66–76 Complete this timetable. Each lesson begins when the previous one ends.

	Lesson starts	Length of lesson	Lesson finishes
	08.55	35 minutes	09.30
	09.30	40 minutes	10.10
	10.10	25 minutes	10.35
Break	10.35	15 minutes	10.50
	10.50	35 minutes	11.25
	11.25	35 minutes	12.00

77–82 Underline the words which have their letters in alphabetical order.
bacon lost adder dish bowl accent blot blind
blow syrup film

Underline the correct answer in each line.

83 If **xpvmy** stands for **medal**, **ymxp** will stand for (deal, meal, lame, laid).

84 If **zstuv** stands for **bread**, **vust** will stand for (bare, read, dare, dear).

85 If **bxyjn** stands for **darts**, **yxjn** will stand for (dart, rats, star, arts).

86 If **acblk** stands for **stone**, **lbck** will stand for (note, tone, nets, nuts).

There are twenty children in a class. Here is a chart which shows how their desks are placed. Each desk is given two numbers (the column number first, then the row number).

Here is where some of the children sit:
John (5, 3), Ann (2, 2), Jamie (5, 1), Mandy (4, 2), Elaine (2, 4).

87–91 Write their names in the correct spaces.

Rows		Columns 1	2	3	4	5
	4	....	Elaine	....	....	....
	3	....	....	....	....	John
	2	....	Ann	....	Mandy	....
	1	....	....	....	....	Jamie
		1	2	3	4	5

Columns

92 Give the number of David's desk if he wants to be sure of having a boy in front of him and a boy behind him. (5, 2)

93 Give the number of Sarah's desk if she is to be sure of having a girl on either side of her. (3, 2)

94 Give the number of Tom's desk if he is to be sure of having a girl in front of him and a girl behind him. (2, 3)

Fill each space with one of these words.

out small ends shoulders blow means

95 head and shoulders

96 odds and ends

97 puff and blow

98 ways and means

99 in and out

100 great and small

Paper 4

In each of the following lines put a ring round the largest number and underline the smallest.

1–2	89	79	88	78	98	97
3–4	314	431	143	134	413	334
5–6	779	978	987	889	789	778
7–8	1578	8571	5178	5718	5781	8751
9–10	4233	4323	3423	3243	2343	3432
11–12	5782	2578	5872	7825	8752	7252

13 If it is 7.10 p.m. now, in how many minutes will it be a quarter to eight? 35

14 I thought of a number and when I added 4 to it the answer was 16. What is half the number I first thought of? 6

15 A row of houses is numbered 2, 4, 6, 8, 10 and so on. If the last number is 24, how many houses are there in the row? 12

16 My watch, which is five minutes fast, shows that it is seven minutes past three o'clock. What is the right time? 3.02

Complete each line by underlining a word in the brackets.

17 Monday is to Tuesday as May is to (April, March, June, July)

18 Gloves are to hands as socks are to (shoes, tights, feet)

19 Minute is to hour as 1 is to (2, 12, 24, 60)

20 Sailor is to navy as soldier is to (captain, army, tank, gun)

21 Baker is to bread as butcher is to (pork, beef, meat, shop)

One word in each line cannot be formed from the letters of the word on the left, using each letter once only. Underline that word.

22	**custard**	sad	last	dust	card	acts
23	**spaghetti**	get	hat	past	great	sight
24	**currant**	tar	can	car	rat	tin
25	**pudding**	pug	nip	gap	din	did
26	**bread**	dare	dad	bed	ear	dear
27	**sprouts**	sour	stop	prod	tour	ours

From the list on the left-hand side of the page choose the word which will best fill each space.

28–34 Write the number of that word in the brackets.

thimble (1)	Amanda had sent out the ..(4).. to her
jellies (2)	..(3).. party, and now she was helping
Christmas (3)	her ..(7).. to get ready for the great
invitations (4)	day. "Let's play 'Hunt the ..(1)..',"
children (5)	said Amanda, "and we can finish with ..(6).."
charades (6)	"I must make plenty of ..(2)..," Mum added.
Mum (7)	"The ..(5).. always enjoy them."

Underline any of the following words which form other words when spelled backwards.

35	dole	dial	dent	doll	dust
36	talk	tent	tint	trip	tool
37	went	wake	ward	walk	wink
38	swab	skin	shoe	stab	slab
39	nook	nuts	nice	neat	nail
40	ease	edge	envy	easy	evil

One day Mum was ill so the twins, Joanna and Joe, decided to cook the lunch which had to be ready by 12.45 p.m. Mum said that the joint of lamb would take $1\frac{1}{2}$ hours to cook, the cauliflower would take a quarter of an hour, the potatoes would take 25 minutes and the gravy would take 10 minutes.

41 They should start cooking the meat at (11.00, 11.15, 11.30, 12.15)

42 They should start cooking the potatoes at (12.00, 12.15, 12.20, 12.25)

43 They should start cooking the cauliflower at (11.45, 11.55, 12.05, 12.30)

44 They should start cooking the gravy at (12.35, 12.40, 12.45, 12.50)

In each line there is a number which is wrong. Underline that number and then write the correct number in the space.

45	65	60	54	50	45	40	..55..
46	72	63	54	45	35	27	..36..
47	32	15	8	4	2	1	..16..
48	12	18	24	30	36	44	..42..
49	0	80	808	8080	80808	808080	..8..

Here is a magic square. Each row, each column and each diagonal adds up to the same number. Fill in the missing numbers.

50–53

8	1	6
3	5	7
4	9	2

a b c d e f g h i j k l m n o p q r s t u v w x y z

Tony thought of a code for writing secret letters to his friends. It was very simple. He used the letter in the alphabet just before the one he wanted. For example **come** would be written **bnld**. How would Tony write:

54–57 Where is my book?

Vgdqd hr lx annj?

The following words are written in the same code. What do they mean?

58–62 Hs hr nm sgd cdrj

It is on the desk

You can change **call** into **fail** by changing one letter on each line like this:

c a l l
f a l l
f a i l

Can you do these?

63	64	65	66
c a r d	p a l e	b a l l	m e a t
h a r d	s a l e	b e l l	p e a t
h a r m	s a l t	s e l l	p e a k

Charlotte is twice as old as Rachel and Ann is 2 years younger than Charlotte. Ann is 10 years old.

67 Who is the youngest? (Anne, Rachel, Charlotte)

68 Who is the eldest? (Anne, Rachel, Charlotte)

69 How old was Rachel 3 years ago? 3 years

70 How old will Anne be in 4 years time? 14 years

Samantha and Sally have fair hair, and Sally and Anne have blue eyes. Samantha and Sheila have brown eyes, and Sheila and Anne have black hair.

71 Who has fair hair and brown eyes? ......Samantha......

72 Who has black hair and brown eyes? ......Sheila......

73 Who has fair hair and blue eyes? ......Sally......

74 Who has black hair and blue eyes? ......Anne......

Below are listed some of the things done by George each morning. Number them as he would do them, starting with the first.

75 George has breakfast. ....3....

76 George walks to school. ....5....

77 George wakes up. ....1....

78 George starts his lessons. ....6....

79 George puts on his overcoat. ....4....

80 George gets up. ....2....

In each line write the opposite of the word underlined. All the answers begin with the letters **sh**.

81 The soldier was very <u>tall.</u> sh....ort....

82 They <u>whispered</u> to each other. sh....outed....

83 The lake was very <u>deep.</u> sh....allow....

84 <u>He</u> met John on the way to school. sh....e....

85 They found the door was <u>open.</u> sh....ut....

86 When her friends came in she <u>hid</u> her presents. sh....owed....

87 If the day before yesterday was Tuesday, what day is it tomorrow?
......Friday......

88 What are the three middle letters of the third month? ......arc......

89 Which month starts with the fourteenth letter of the alphabet?
......November......

90 Which month has the fewest days? ......February......

91 Which month has most letters in its name? ......September......

92 Which is the eighth month of the year? ......August......

A test was set for children who were born between 1st September 1972 and 31st August 1973. Would the children below take the test?

93 Mark was born on 31st December, 1972. (Yes, no)

94 Sara was born on 1st September, 1973. (Yes, no)

95 Lucy was born on 30th August, 1972. (Yes, no)

96 Andrew was born on 30th April, 1973. (Yes, no)

Put in alphabetical order:

potato radish onion parsnip

97 (1) onion .... 98 (2) parsnip ....

99 (3) potato .... 100 (4) radish ....

Paper 5

One drawing in each line is "odd one out". Decide which it is, and draw a line underneath it.

1
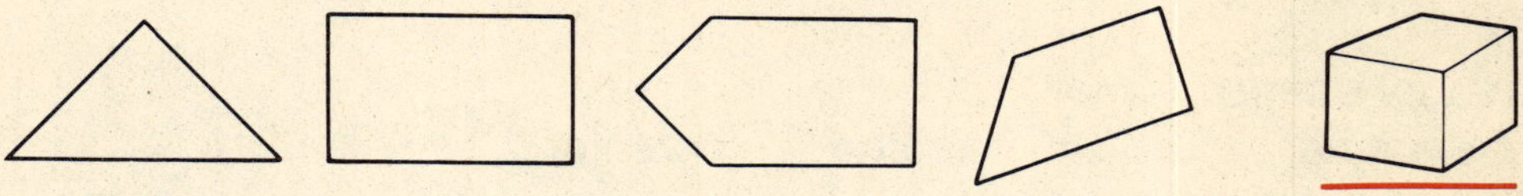

2
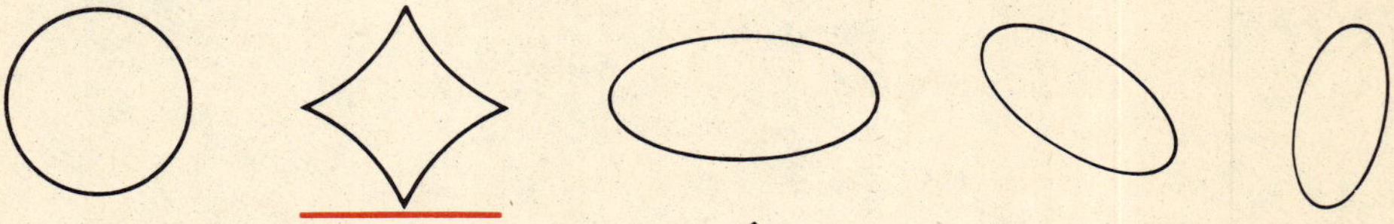

3
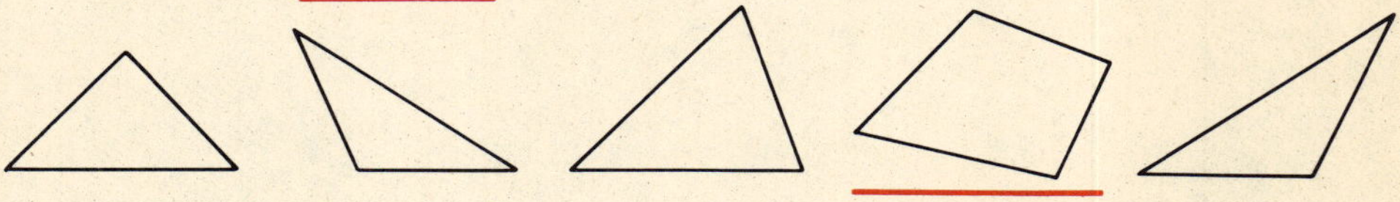

4

5
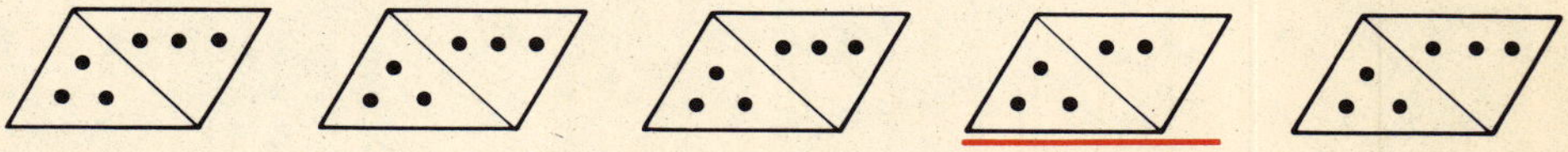

6
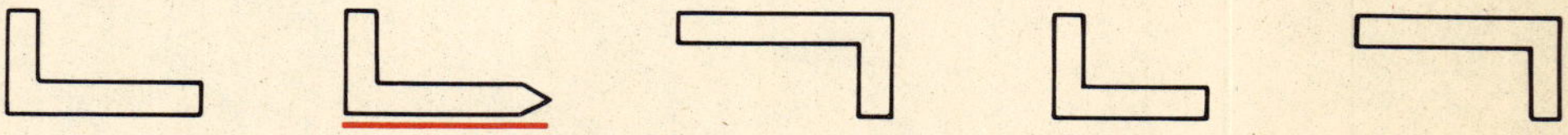

Use the words below to fill in the spaces.

teeth finger nose eye shoulder

7 Emma didn't like fish and she turned up her ......nose...... when her mother gave her a kipper for breakfast.

8 The new boy was not popular, and the class gave him the cold ......shoulder......

9 When he fell off his bicycle he escaped being run over by the skin of his ......teeth......

10 Mum knew that Tim would keep an ......eye...... on his small brother.

11 She liked history and had details of the Kings and Queens at her ......finger......tips.

Two words in each line are formed from the same letters. Underline both words.

12–13	piano	plate	plays	pedal	petal
14–15	shall	house	shore	homes	horse
16–17	chair	chest	table	blame	bleat

18 You would find the date from
(an atlas, a timetable, a calendar, a directory)

19 You would find the time of a train from
(a diary, an atlas, a newspaper, a timetable)

20 You would find the meaning of a word from
(a dictionary, the Radio Times, a directory, a diary)

21 You would find details of TV programmes from
(a directory, the Radio Times, a timetable, an atlas)

Here is another code. The signs are not under the right words. Can you sort them out?

m a n	a n d	m e n	a n
○⊡□	○△□	△□	△□⊙

22 **man** should be ○△□ ....

23 **and** should be △□⊙ ....

24 **men** should be ○⊡□ ....

25 **an** should be △□ ....

26 In this code how would **mend** be written? ○⊡□⊙ ....

27 In this code how would **mane** be written? ○△□⊡ ....

If 2 bananas and 2 oranges cost 34p and 2 bananas and 1 orange cost 25p:

28 What is the cost of one banana? 8p

29 What is the cost of one orange? 9p

Underline any of the following words which begin and end with the same letter.

30–32	start	twist	motor	razor	hunch
33–34	going	skill	swing	broad	ruler
35–36	puppy	level	never	toast	minor

Mr. Young was 25 when John was born.

37–44 Fill in the correct ages in the chart below.

Mr. Young's age	27	30	35	37	40	45	50	55
John's age	2	5	10	12	15	20	25	30

Write these words in alphabetical order.

down dale duck deed dice

45 (1) dale 46 (2) deed

47 (3) dice 48 (4) down

49 (5) duck

In each line there are two drawings which are not in the correct order. Underline them.

50–51 

52–53 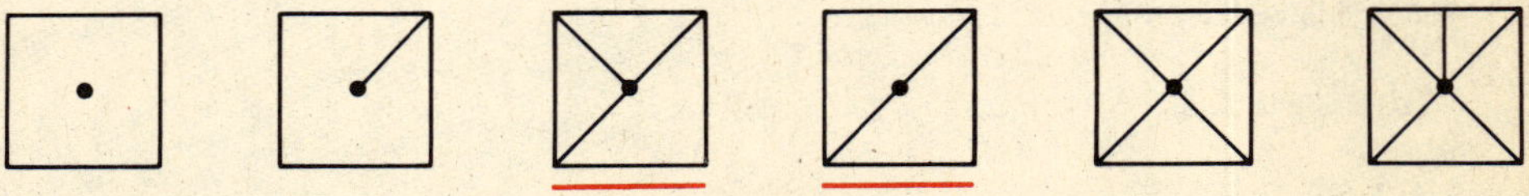

54–55 

Use the following to fill the spaces below.

peacock horse bee owl dove bat mouse

56 As busy as a bee 57 As quiet as a mouse

58 As blind as a bat 59 As wise as an owl

60 As strong as a horse 61 As proud as a peacock

62 As gentle as a dove

Underline the correct word in the brackets.

63 My mother's sister is my (sister, aunt, grandmother, son).

64 My uncle's child is my (cousin, brother, sister, aunt).

65 My cousin's mother is my (grandmother, cousin, sister, aunt).

66 My father's father is my (son, grandfather, brother, uncle).

67 My father's brother is my (son, brother, uncle, aunt).

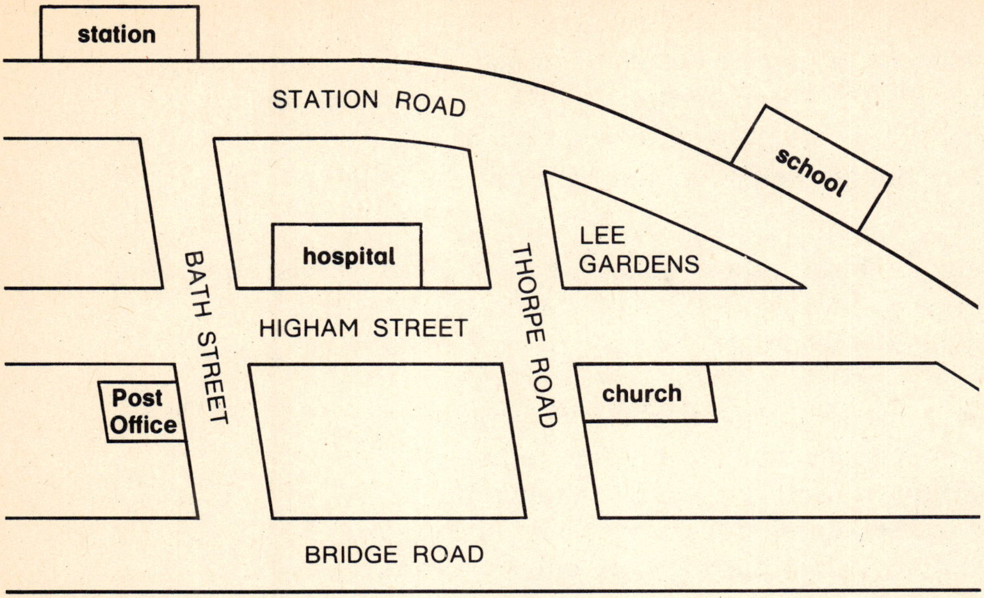

68 Alison lives at the corner of Higham Street and Bath Street. The (station, hospital, school, church) is nearest to her house.

69 Ben lives on the corner of Bridge Road and Thorpe Road. He is nearest to the (station, hospital, school, church).

70 Which of these buildings is south of Lee Gardens? (Station, hospital, school, church)

71 The hospital is on (Station Road, Bath Street, Higham Street, Bridge Road).

72 Which of these is nearest to Lee Gardens? (Station, school, hospital, Post Office)

73 The Post Office is on (Bridge Road, Bath Street, Thorpe Road, Station Road).

In each of the following lines there are six words. One of these words describes four of the other words. Underline that word and draw a ring round the word which doesn't fit in with the others.

74–75	orange	lemon	fruit	banana	grape	cake
76–77	Edward	Sally	George	William	Kings	Henry
78–79	country	England	France	Wales	London	Italy
80–81	robin	bird	wren	thrush	cat	sparrow
82–83	ten	twenty	one	hundred	second	number
84–85	August	January	April	Monday	May	month

86–93 Can you work out what these jumbled words really are?
Tim and his parents were having a holiday in **oonndl** London
After having a good breakfast of **cnoab** bacon and **gesg** eggs, **tstao** toast and **uerttb** butter, and either **fefeco** coffee or **ate** tea to drink, they went out to see the sights. First they went to Buckingham Palace to see the changing of the **adurg** Guard

94 Anthony is three years younger than Barbara who is a year older than Colin who is twelve. How old is Anthony? 10

95 How old is Barbara? 13

96 What is the middle letter of the word **abundance**? d

97 How many consonants are there in the word? 5

98 How many vowels are there in the word? 4

99 How many letters appear more than once? 2

100 How many letters appear once only? 5

Paper 6

856 654 685 556 436

1 Which of the above numbers can be divided by 5? 685

2 Which number can be divided by 3? 654

3 Which is the smallest number? 436

4 Which number can be divided by 6? 654

5 Which is the largest number? 856

Underline the drawing in the brackets which would be the next drawing in the series on the left of the page.

6 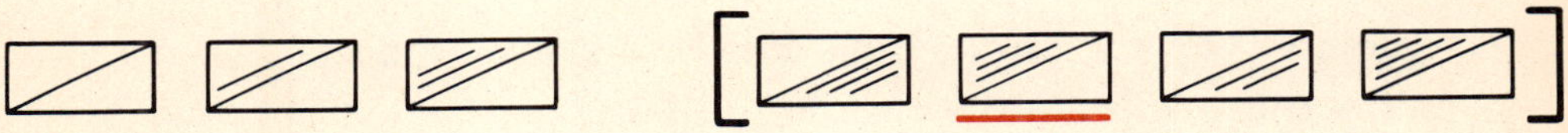

7 

8 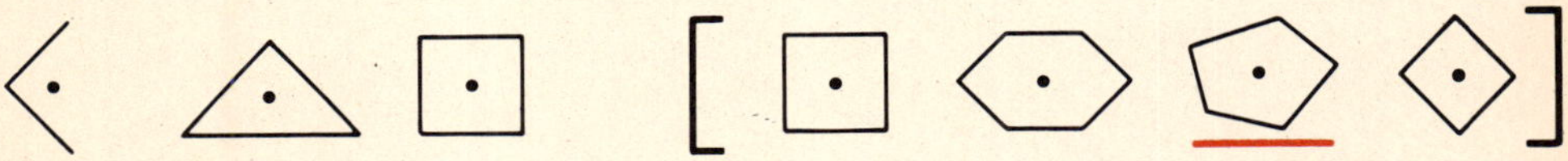

9 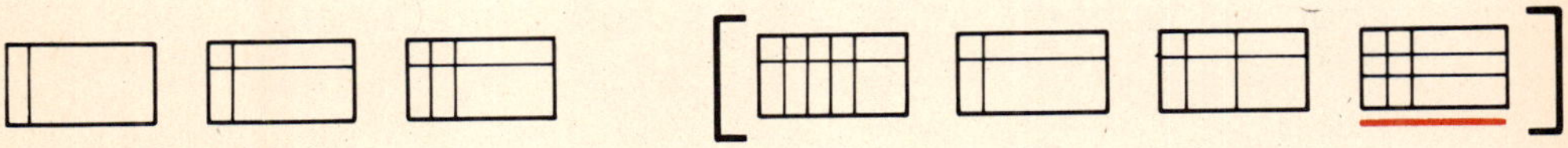

10 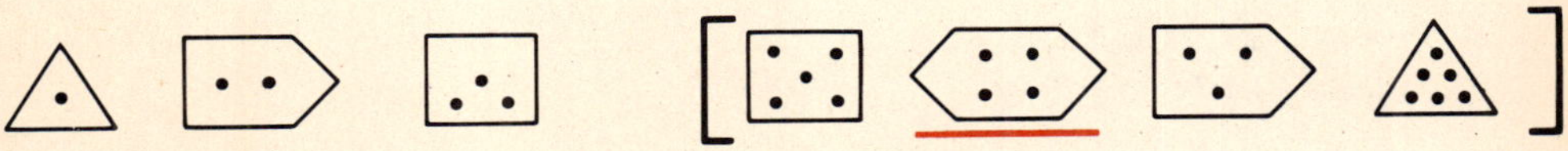

11 

12 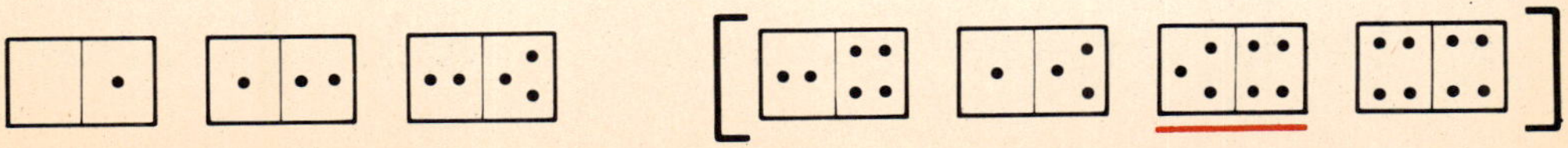

Underline any of the following words in which all the letters are different.

13–18 manuscript submarine describe creation feather
thirsty discharge generous grateful leopard

Town	Distance from London
Birmingham	181 km
Bath	171 km
Bournemouth	173 km
Chester	288 km
Exeter	275 km
Bristol	189 km
Cardiff	245 km

19 Which town is the greatest distance from London? Chester

20 Which town is the nearest to London? Bath

21 Which town is 30 km farther from London than Cardiff? Exeter

22 Which town is 10 km nearer to London than Birmingham? Bath

23 Which town is 16 km nearer London than Bristol? Bournemouth

24 Which town is 8 km farther from London than Birmingham? Bristol

25 The church is due east of our house and our house is due east of the school. In what direction is the school from the church? west

Alison is 10 years old. She is twice as old as her cousin, Timothy, who is 3 years younger than his brother David.

26 How old is Timothy? 5 years

27 How old is David? 8 years

1 2 3 4 5 6 7 8 9 10 11 12 13

28 Add together the first and third odd numbers. 6

29 Take the smallest odd number from the largest even number. 11

30 Take the smallest even number from the largest odd number. 11

Here are the signs of the Zodiac and their dates.

Aquarius	January 21–February 19
Pisces	February 20–March 20
Aries	March 21–April 20
Taurus	April 21–May 21
Gemini	May 22–June 21
Cancer	June 22–July 23
Leo	July 24–August 23
Virgo	August 24–September 23
Libra	September 24–October 23
Scorpio	October 24–November 22
Sagittarius	November 23–December 22
Capricorn	December 23–January 20

31 A person born on January 13th is born under the sign of (Aquarius, Leo, Capricorn, Sagittarius)

32 Dad's birthday is on May 17th so he was born under the sign of (Taurus, Gemini, Pisces)

33 Christmas Day comes under the sign of (Aquarius, Sagittarius, Capricorn)

34 My birthday is on August 30th. My sign is (Leo, Virgo, Cancer)

35 February 1st is under the sign of (Aquarius, Capricorn, Pisces)

I was helping to plan our Christmas menu. In a cookery book I found out that:

a 3 kg turkey serves 6–8 people
a 5 kg turkey serves 10–12 people
a 6 kg turkey serves 12–16 people

I also read that you should cook a turkey:

50 minutes for each kg for a 3–6 kg turkey
40 minutes for each kg for a 7–8 kg turkey

36 On Christmas Day there will be our family of six people, two aunts, two uncles, one grandfather and three more children. How many people will there be? ..14.. people

37 How big a turkey will we need? a ..6 kg.. turkey

38 How long will it need to be cooked? ..5.. hours ..0.. minutes

39 If we want the turkey ready at 1.45 p.m. when shall we start cooking it? (6.45, 8.45, 8.30, 10.00)

1 2 3 4 5 6 7 8 9 10 11 12 13

40 What is the sum of the first four even numbers? 20

41 What is the sum of the first four odd numbers? 16

42 What is the product of the greatest and the smallest numbers? 13

At the end of each line fill in the next two numbers.

43–44	2	7	3	8	4	9	5	10
45–46	109	98	87	76	65	54	43	32
47–48	2p	3q	4r	5s	6t	7u	8v	9w

In each line one of the words in the column on the left is the opposite of one of the words in the column on the right. Underline both words.

49–50	length, high, metre	low, small, bottom
51–52	saw, up, went	walk, go, down
53–54	clothes, pretty, young	dress, old, woman

55–57 Write down the numbers from ten to sixteen. Then put a line through the middle odd number and put a ring round the smallest even number. Underline the largest odd number.

(10) 11 12 ~~13~~ 14 15 16

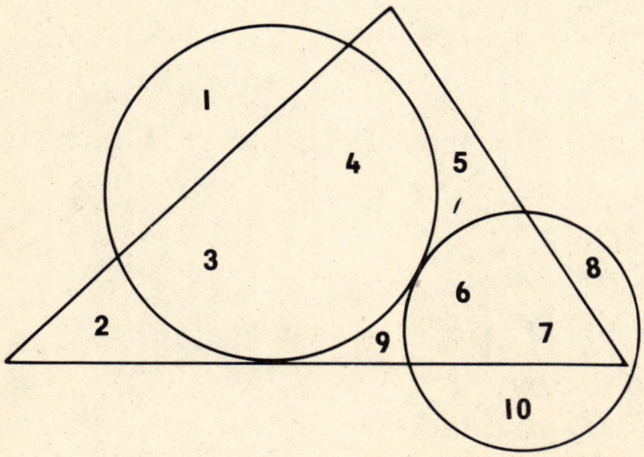

In the above diagram:

58–59 Which numbers are in the large circle and also in the triangle? 3 and 4

60–61 Which numbers are in the small circle and also in the triangle? 6 and 7

62 Which number is in the large circle only? 1

63–64 Which numbers are in the small circle only? 8 and 10

65–67 Which numbers are in the triangle only? 2, 5, 9

length area centimetre metre measure

68 Which word contains the fewest vowels? length

69 Which word has only one consonant? area

70 Which letter is found twice in **measure** and once in **length**? e

71 Which word contains the eighth letter of the alphabet? length

72 Which letter is found most often in all these words put together? e

73 If the words were put in dictionary order which would be the second word? centimetre

74 Which would be the last word? metre

Choose a word from the column on the right to complete each line and write the number of the word in the brackets.

75	A hundred years is a (7)	(1)	animal
76	A person who writes books is an (3)	(2)	artist
77	A person who paints pictures is an (2)	(3)	author
78	A person who designs houses is an (5)	(4)	season
79	A mule is an (1)	(5)	architect
80	An ant is an (6)	(6)	insect
81	Autumn is a (4)	(7)	century

Here is another code. The number of kg or packets tells you the number of the letter to use from each word.
Example: 4 kg of potatoes – the 4th letter of **potatoes** is **a**.
Remember – only count the letters of the last word in each line.
Underline the letters and then write the message below.

82 3 kg of spinach
83 1 loaf
84 2 kg of mince
85 5 large steaks
86 6 oranges
87 7 pkts of custard
88 4 kg of sprouts
89 1 pkt of gelatine
90 1 tin of soup
91 I like dogs

92 What letter is in **Sunday** but not in **Tuesday**? .... n

93 What letter is in **July** but not in **January**? l

94 What letter in the word **December** has the same position in the word as it has in the alphabet? c

95 What letter in the word **Monday** has the same position in the word as it has in the alphabet? .... d

96 How many months of the year end with the letters **-ember**? 3

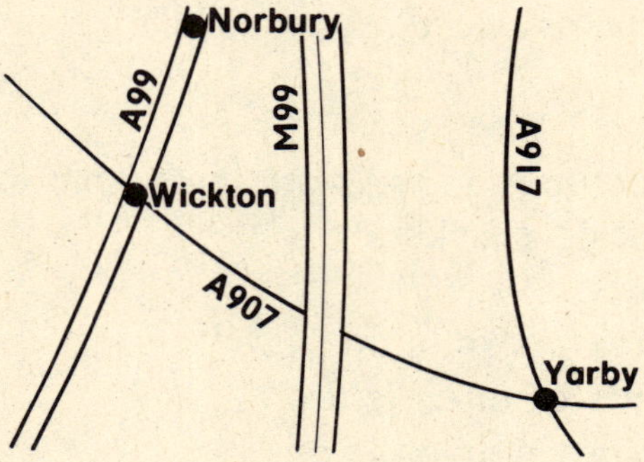

97 Norbury is on the (M99, A99, A907, A917)

98 Yarby is at the junction of the (A917 and A907, A917 and A99, A907 and M99)

99 Wickton is at the junction of the (A907 and M99, A917 and A907, A907 and A99)

100 The quickest way from Norbury to Yarby is by the (A917 and A99, A99 and A907)

Paper 7

1 Underline the number which can be divided exactly by 4.
(342, 256, 114)

2 Underline the number which can be divided exactly by 5.
(556, 371, 145)

3 Underline the number which can be divided exactly by 6.
(252, 662, 363)

Underline the correct word in the brackets.

4 All libraries have (people, chairs, books, tables)

5 All dresses have (skirts, buttons, belts, sleeves)

6 All hands have (gloves, chilblains, rings, fingers)

7 All bicycles have (saddlebags, wheels, pumps, sheds)

8 All trousers have (shorts, belts, legs, braces)

9 All soldiers have (uniforms, guns, tanks, battles)

10 All days have (sunshine, rain, hours, snow)

11 What is the answer when you take the largest even number less than ten from the largest odd number less than ten? ....1....

Four children made plasticine models.
Sandra and Jane chose green plasticine.
Martin and Janice chose blue plasticine.
Toby and Jason chose red plasticine.

Jason and Jane made pigs.
Toby and Janice made giraffes.
Sandra and Martin made elephants.

12 Who made a blue elephant? ....Martin....

13 Who made a red giraffe? ....Toby....

14 Who made a green pig? ....Jane....

15 Who made a blue giraffe? ....Janice....

16 Who made a red pig? ....Jason....

17 Who made a green elephant? ....Sandra....

In each of the next three lines there are two words which have similar meanings. Underline those words.

18–19	unite	under	push	join	power	depart
20–21	wander	upstairs	terror	fear	grope	lean
22–23	untidy	neat	modern	worn	old	new

24–27 Underline any of the following words which have no two letters the same.

manager	Saturday	Scotland	teacher
cushion	sandwich	exercise	cupboard

Prime Ministers	
Duke of Wellington	1828–1830
Disraeli	1874–1880
Robert Walpole	1727–1742
Sir Robert Peel	1834–1835
William Pitt	1783–1801
William Gladstone (1st time)	1868 – 1874

King or Queen	
George II	1727–1760
George III	1760–1820
George IV	1820–1830
William IV	1830–1837
Victoria	1837–1901

28 The Duke of Wellington was Prime Minister in George IV's reign.
29 Disraeli was Prime Minister in Victoria's reign.
30 Robert Walpole was Prime Minister in George II's reign.
31 Sir Robert Peel was Prime Minister in William IV's reign.
32 William Pitt was Prime Minister in George III's reign.
33 William Gladstone was Prime Minister in Victoria's reign.

Jonathan is twice as old as his sister Kim who was three two years ago. Kim is four years younger than Peter.

34 How old is Jonathan now? 10
35 How old is Kim now? 5
36 How old is Peter now? 9
37 How old was Jonathan when Kim was born? 5
38 How old was Peter when Kim was born? 4

This chart shows you how much it costs to stay in Naples or Athens.

	May		June/July		August	
	7 days	14 days	7 days	14 days	7 days	14 days
Naples	£130	£160	£140	£170	£155	£185
Athens	£155	£190	£170	£200	£180	£215

39 A week in June in Naples would cost (£130, £140, £160, £155)

40 How much more would it cost to spend a week in Athens in August than in May? £25

41 It costs as much to spend a fortnight in Naples in June/July as it does to spend a week in Athens in (August, May, June/July)

42 How much does it cost to spend 2 weeks in Athens in August? (£190, £200, £180, £215)

43 It costs as much to spend a week in Athens in May as it does to spend a week in Naples in (May, June/July, August)

44 How much would it cost for 2 people to spend a fortnight in Naples in July? £340

One word in each line has a completely different meaning from the others. Underline the word that is out of place.

45	normal	usual	increase	common	average
46	pain	hurt	ache	sore	healthy
47	push	weight	force	heave	lift
48	clear	bright	sunny	weather	beautiful
49	relation	uncle	aunt	sister	brother
50	clatter	crackle	silence	hiss	squelch

i	m	p	o	r	t	a	n	c	e
m	a	n	u	s	c	r	i	p	t

Here is another code. The letters of the word **importance** are changed when writing in code to the letters of the word **manuscript**.

51–53 Write in code:

Come at once

Puat rc uipt

54–59 The following words are written in code. What are they?

M pri attc nrc rc cti

I can meet Pat at ten

Complete each line by underlining the correct words in brackets.

60–61 Today is to yesterday as (May, June, July) is to (August, May, March)

62–63 Two is to hands as (four, five, ten) is to (toes, hands, thumbs)

64–65 Roof is to house as (ceiling, window, wall) is to (cover, room, floor)

Choose from the list on the right something which is used by each of the following people in their work.

66	butcher	chopper	medicine
67	doctor	medicine	flex
68	carpenter	hammer	spade
69	gardener	spade	cheques
70	bank manager	cheques	chalk
71	painter	brush	chopper
72	builder	bricks	bricks
73	teacher	chalk	brush
74	tailor	needle	hammer
75	electrician	flex	needle

In the following sums fill in the missing figures.

76–77
```
  3 4 3 2
+ 6 2 8 8
---------
  9 7 2 0
```

78–79
```
  7 2
- 3 7
-----
  3 5
```

80–81
```
  3 2 8
+ 2 8 4
-------
  6 1 2
```

82–83
```
  7 1 6 8
- 3 9 2 5
---------
  3 2 4 3
```

84–85
```
  2 4
×   8
-----
1 9 2
```

86–87
```
    2 2 6
2 ) 4 5 2
```

Use the words below to complete the following sayings.

black   sweet   red   clear   warm   brown

88 As warm as wool

89 As brown as a berry

90 As clear as daylight

91 As red as a beetroot

92 As black as night

93 As sweet as sugar

Put these names in the order in which you would find them in a telephone directory.

Smith J.W. Smith L.C. Smith J.M. Smith J.L.
Smith K. Smith L.A. Smith K.K.

94 (1) Smith J.L.

95 (2) Smith J.M.

96 (3) Smith J.W.

97 (4) Smith K.

98 (5) Smith K.K.

99 (6) Smith L.A.

100 (7) Smith L.C.

Paper 8

Two drawings on each line are different from the others. Underline the ones that are different.

1–2 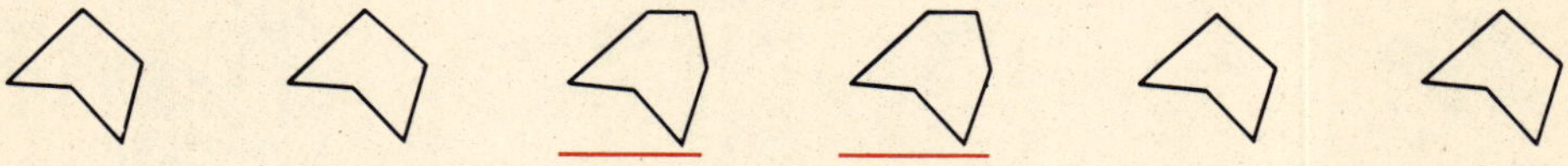

3–4 

5–6 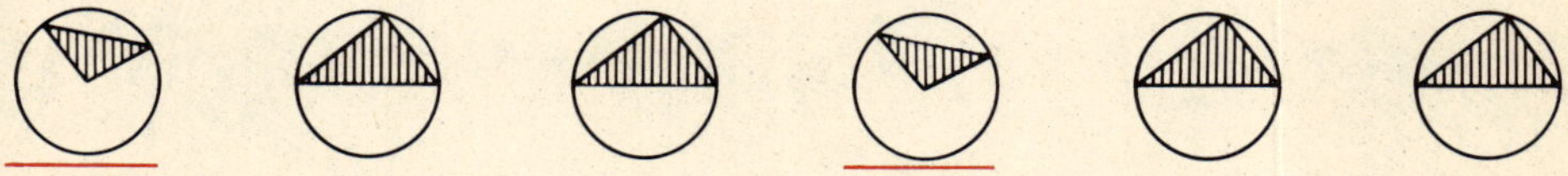

The words in heavy type have been jumbled. Write the correct word in the space.

7 The **soyb** were very excited. They had just heard .... boys
8 that they could go to the **rfia** which had .... fair
9 arrived on the **mcomon**. They took their .... common
10 pocket **oenmy** with them as they wanted to go on .... money
11 the roundabouts and the **shotg** train. "Come on," said .... ghost
12 Daniel, "let's buy a **llooanb**." "All right," said Shaun, ... balloon
13 who was feeling very pleased as he had **onw** .... won
14–15 a **foldgish** on the coconut **alstl**. .... goldfish .... stall

In each line there are two words formed from the same letters. Underline both the words.

16–17	shoot	those	hoots	these	shots
18–19	stole	tales	skate	steer	slate
20–21	stare	tasty	taste	state	steak

Write the next word in each line.

22	some	same	dome	dame	tome	tame
23	four	hour	fang	hang	feat	heat
24	lair	hair	lint	hint	lost	host
25	clan	clean	dram	dream	chap	cheap
26	pace	place	sing	sling	back	black
27	creep	cheep	prone	phone	trick	thick

28–33 Six families live in a small road called Riverside Road. Read about them below, and then write their names in the houses.
The Smiths live in a house which has an odd number.
The Greys live opposite the Browns.
The Patels live opposite the Smiths.
The Scotts are on the same side as the Smiths but not next door to them.
The Greens and the Greys live in houses with even numbers.
The Patels' garden stretches down to the river.

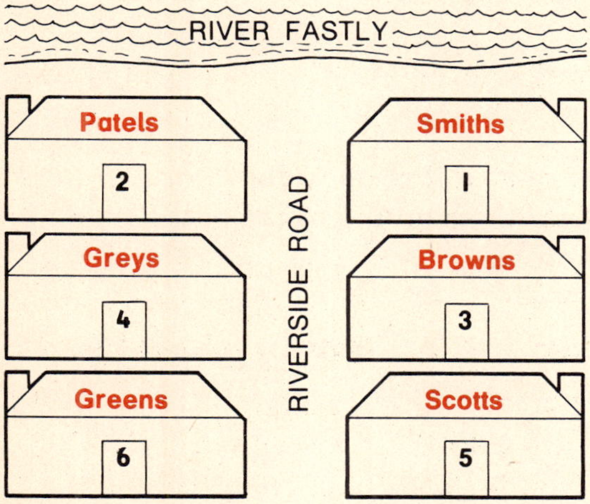

The words below are written in a number code. The numbers are not always under the right words.

want	ant	tan	tank
5742	745	574	9745

The right pairings are:

34 want 9745 .... 35 ant 745 .... 36 tan 574 .... 37 tank 5742 ....

38 In this code it would be possible for **bank** to be (5274, 3742, 4745)
39 **Ten** could be (715, 514, 924)

40 Fiona was born in 1972. I am 4 years younger. I was born in (1968, 1976, 1975, 1972)
41 Gary was born in March 1977, and David was born in March 1976. Who is the elder? David ....
42 Helen is my cousin so her father is my (brother, uncle, father, cousin)

a b c d e f g h i j k l m n o p q r s t u v w x y z

43 If **a**, **b** and **c** were taken out of the alphabet, what would be the 10th letter? m

44 How many letters would there be in this alphabet? 23

45 Which is the middle letter of the word **dexterity**? e

46–47 Which letters in the word **dexterity** appear more than once? e and t

48 If **dexterity** was spelled backwards which would be the 7th letter? x

49 If the letters of the word **bread** were put in alphabetical order which would be the middle letter? d

50 If the alphabet was written backwards (starting at **z**) which would be the 17th letter? j

51–58 It is noon in some countries before it is noon here, and in other countries it is later. In Slowvia their time is 40 minutes behind our time. Complete the following chart.

Time in Britain	09.30	10.00	11.50	12.40	13.20	14.55	16.30	18.00
Time in Slowvia	08.50	09.20	11.10	12.00	12.40	14.15	15.50	17.20

In each of the following lines put a ring round the middle quantity or middle thing.

59	cold	cool	warm	hot	freezing
60	Wednesday	Monday	Friday	Thursday	Tuesday
61	378	873	387	738	783
62	tiny	small	gigantic	large	medium
63	$\frac{1}{3}$	$\frac{1}{2}$	$\frac{2}{3}$	$\frac{3}{4}$	$\frac{1}{4}$
64	toddler	grandfather	baby	father	boy
65	4 × 7	9 × 3	6 × 4	5 × 5	8 × 4
66	$1\frac{1}{2}$	2·5	2	3	1
67	50p	2 for £2·00	75p	4 for £1·00	£1·25
68	happy	delighted	cross	furious	contented
69	January	March	May	April	February

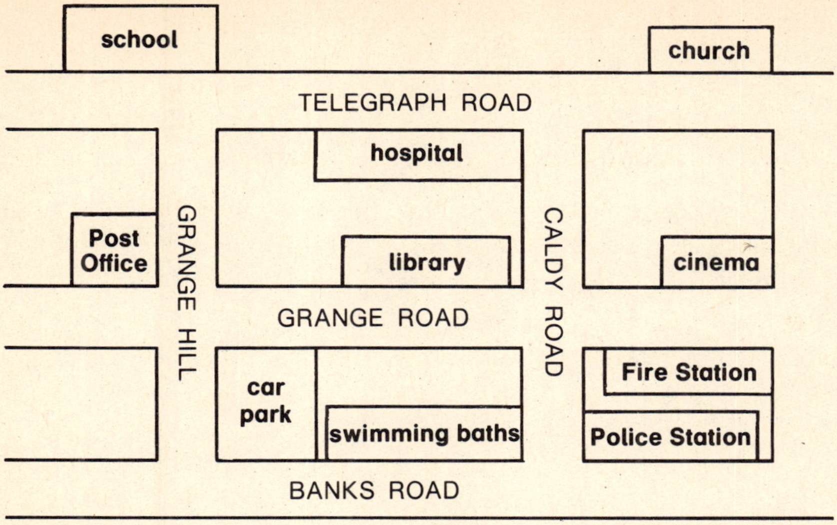

70 Which of these is not on Telegraph Road?
(Hospital, cinema, school, church)

71 Which is not on Grange Road?
(Post Office, cinema, library, Police Station)

72 Which is nearest to the Police Station?
(Fire Station, cinema, school, Post Office)

73 The car park is not on:
(Grange Road, Caldy Road, Grange Hill, Banks Road)

Change the first word to the second by changing one letter at a time.

74 stay
slay
slam

75 that
chat
chap

76 cast
past
pass

77 fire
dire
dirt

78 duck
luck
lack

Underline the word in the brackets which has the closest connection with the words on the left of the page.

79	cat, horse, sheep	(fish, frog, beetle, dog)
80	Samantha, Sally, Sandra	(Jane, Suzanna, Karen, Lisa)
81	cathedral, chapel, abbey	(cinema, church, town hall, palace)
82	36, 60, 108, 72	(55, 45, 24, 20, 82)

Complete the following:

83–84 Skin is to b*anana*.......... as p*eel*.......... is to orange.

85–86 Air is to b*ird*.......... as w*ater*.......... is to fish.

87–88 Rind is to c*heese*.......... as c*rust*.......... is to loaf.

89–90 Ascend is to d*escend*.......... as u*p*.......... is to down.

91–100 Put a line through any letters in the following words which have the same place in the word as they do in the alphabet.

diff~~e~~r ~~a~~s~~c~~end won~~d~~~~e~~r ~~a~~~~b~~sence

en~~c~~ounter ~~a~~udible se~~c~~ond

Paper 9

Complete the following lines by filling in the spaces.

1	96	48	24	12	6	3
2	9	7	8	6	7	5
3	20	22	21	23	22	24
4	1	2	4	5	7	8
5	15	17	14	16	13	15

Complete each of the following lines by underlining a figure or word in the brackets.

6 $\frac{1}{8}$ is to $\frac{1}{4}$ as $\frac{1}{2}$ is to ($\frac{1}{4}$, $\frac{3}{8}$, 1, 2, 4)
7 40 is to 4 as 60 is to (6, 40, 60, 20, 600)
8 7 is to 49 as 5 is to (6, 94, 50, 25, 85)
9 $\frac{1}{3}$ is to 3 as 1 is to (6, 3, 9, 4, 12)
10 6 is to 12 as 72 is to (20, 72, 144, 100)
11 4 is to 20 as 3 is to (9, 15, 18, 20, 4)

These sets of figures stand for the words written below but they are not in the right order. Can you work out which set of figures belongs to which word?

757	537	531	124
ant	dad	and	top

When you know the code write the figures for these words.

12	pat	451	13	apt	541
14	dot	721	15	panda	45375
16	pod	427	17	toad	1257

What words do the following figures stand for in this code?

18	277	odd	19	122	too
20	321	not	21	577	add
22	154	tap	23	4531	pant

Underline any of the following words which contain the same letter three times.

24–28 energetic swimming envelope vegetable Saturday
aeroplane balloons beginning electricity pineapple

On each line there are three pairs of words. Underline the pair of words which have opposite meanings.

29	halt/stop	broad/wide	cheap/expensive
30	conceal/hide	rough/smooth	shut/close
31	sour/bitter	hope/help	bent/straight
32	near/far	modern/new	show/display
33	roam/wander	sell/buy	stern/strict
34	tested/tried	rapid/quick	come/go
35	gap/hole	ally/friend	here/there

36 I thought of a number and when I doubled it the result was 4 less than 20. What was the number? 8 ....

37 When I added 5 to a number it was then 6 less than 24. What number did I think of? 13 ....

38 The classroom clock which is five minutes fast shows that it is 8 minutes past 3 o'clock. What is the right time? 3.03 ....

A coach gives 20-minute swimming lessons. How many lessons can he give in 2 hours? 6 ....

40 A clock only strikes the number of hours. How many times does it strike between 12.30 p.m. and 5.30 p.m.? 5 ....

41 Underline which is the longer: $2\frac{1}{2}$ hours or 160 minutes

42 By how much is it longer? 10 min ....

43–46 In the line of figures below cross out all the 5s unless they are next to an even number.

7 8 6 5 4 3 5 7 9 5 1 6 5 4 3 5 7 9 5 1

47–51 In the line of figures below cross out all the even numbers unless they are divisible by 3.

14 17 28 19 21 30 40 23 45 24 26 42 37 16 36

In each of the following lines there are two words which are similar but which are different from the other words. Underline the two words which are different.

52–53	skip	lead	walk	run	iron	jump
54–55	lake	river	mountain	ocean	sea	hill
56–57	cross	kind	generous	good	angry	loving
58–59	red	colour	blue	green	tint	yellow

In each of the following lines one thing is different from the other things on that line. Underline it.

60 37337 37337 37337 33737 37337

61 prbp prbp pbrp prbp prbp

62 69fe 69fe 69fe 69fe 69ff

63
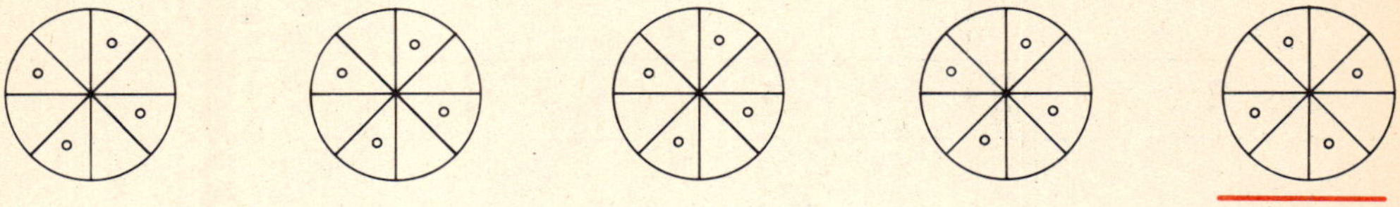

64
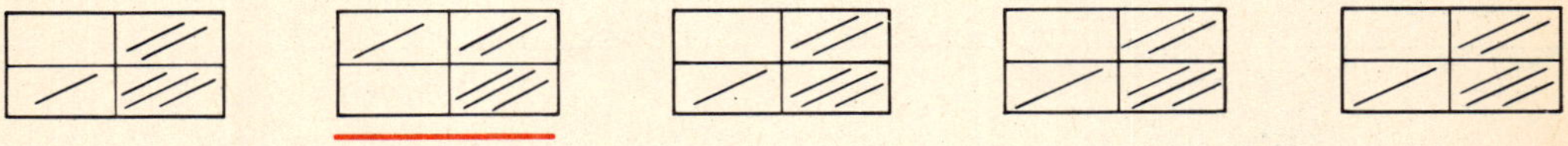

65
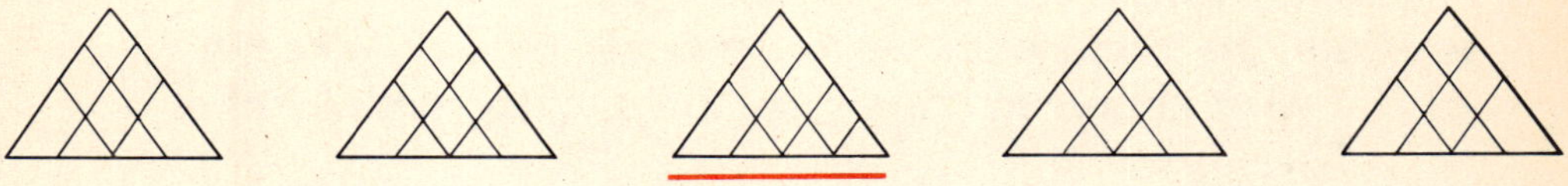

The pegs on one side of a cloakroom are numbered 1 to 10, and on the other side 11 to 20. They are arranged so that 1 is opposite to 20 and 2 opposite to 19.

66 Which peg is opposite No. 4? ...17...

67 Which peg is opposite No. 18? ...3...

68 Which peg is opposite No. 11? ...10...

69 Which peg is opposite No. 13? ...8...

70 Which peg is opposite No. 7? ...14...

10% is another way of saying 10 out of every 100. As a fraction this would be $\frac{1}{10}$. To find $\frac{1}{10}$ of a number you move the decimal point 1 place to the left.

71 10% of £5·70 = ...57p...

72 10% of £12·50 = ...£1·25...

73 10% of £1·20 = ...12p...

74 10% of £37·00 = ...£3·70...

75 10% of £3·80 = ...38p...

76 10% of £21·00 = ...£2·10...

Put these names in the order in which you would find them in a telephone directory.

B.J. White D. Young G. Watson R. Weston H. Wood

77 (1) ...G. Watson...

78 (2) ...R. Weston...

79 (3) ...B.J. White...

80 (4) ...H. Wood...

81 (5) ...D. Young...

A certain airline runs the following flights from these four airports.

Flights to	Flights from Luton	Heathrow	Birmingham	Manchester	Details on page
Majorca	✓	✓	✓	✓	12
Malta	✓	✓	✓	✓	16
Costa Brava	✓			✓	20
Rome		✓		✓	24
Ibiza		✓		✓	29

82 Is there a flight from Birmingham to Malta? (Yes, no)
83 Can I fly from Luton to Rome? (Yes, no)
84 Can I go from Heathrow to the Costa Brava? (Yes, no)
85 On what page can I find details of flights from Manchester to Malta? Page ..16..
86 If I look on page ..29.. I will find out times of flights from Heathrow to Ibiza.
87 Which airport has flights to all five places? (Luton, Heathrow, Birmingham, Manchester)

Here are some of the winners of the Women's Singles at Wimbledon.

1966 Billie-Jean King
1967 Billie-Jean King
1968 Billie-Jean King
1969 Anne Hayden-Jones
1970 Margaret Court
1971 Evonne Goolagong
1972 Billie-Jean King
1973 Billie-Jean King
1974 Christine Evert
1975 Billie-Jean King
1976 Christine Evert

88 Who won the championship the most times? ..Billie-Jean King..
89 How many times did she win it? ..6.. times
90 Who won it the next most times? ..Christine Evert..
91 How many times did she win it? ..2.. times
92 How many of these people won it only once during the period 1966–1976? ..3.. people

Have you tried multiplying by 50 in your head? It is quite easy. All you do is to add two noughts to the number, and then divide it by 2.

Example: $4624 \times 50 = 462\,400 \div 2 = 231\,200$

Do the same with these numbers.

93 $668 \times 50 =$ 33 400

94 $808 \times 50 =$ 40 400

95 $486 \times 50 =$ 24 300

96 $6006 \times 50 =$ 300 300

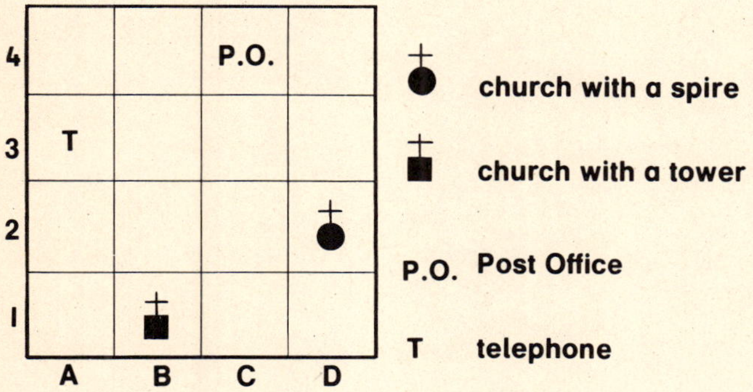

97 In which square is there a church with a tower? B1

98 A church with a spire is in D2

99 The Post Office is in C4

100 The telephone is in A3

Paper 10

1 

2 

3 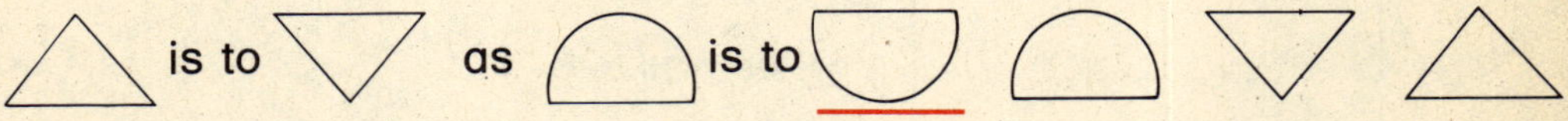

4 

5 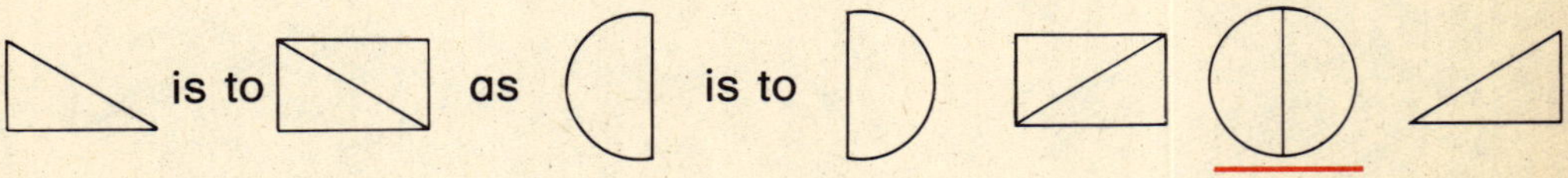

In a code the word **parent** is written **123456**.

How would you write the following words in this code?

6 part 1236 7 pane 1254 8 near 5423 9 tent 6456

What are the following words?

10 5426 neat 11 3421 reap 12 45643 enter 13 2342 area

14 If I had paid 3p more for the book I would have spent a quarter of my money. The book cost 15p, so how much did I have? 72p

15 If my sister was 2 cm taller she would be 10 cm shorter than my brother who is 1·70 m. How tall is my sister? 1·58 m

Julie is 10 years old, and her brother Simon is half her age. Simon is two years younger than Mark who is half the age of Helen.

16 Who is the eldest? (Julie, Simon, Mark, Helen)
17 Who is the second eldest? (Julie, Simon, Mark, Helen)
18 How old is Mark? (5, 10, 3, 12, 7, 6, 9)
19 How old is Simon? (5, 10, 3, 12, 7, 6, 9)

For four weeks four children made graphs of their scores in tests. Look at the graphs carefully and then answer the questions.

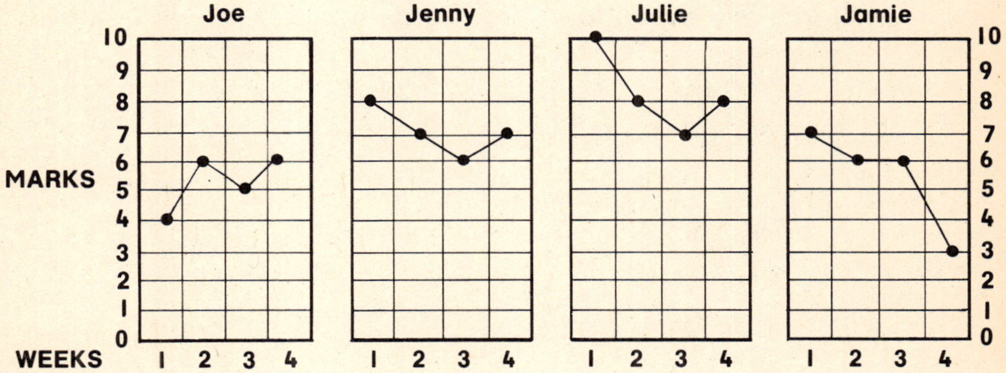

20 How many marks did Joe score in the 4 weeks? 21
21 How many marks did Jenny score altogether in weeks 3 and 4? 13
22 How many marks did Julie score altogether in weeks 1 and 2? 18
23 How many marks did Jamie score altogether in weeks 2 and 3? 12
24 Who hasn't improved at all? Jamie
25 Who got full marks one week? Julie
26 Who got the lowest marks in any test? Jamie

Complete each line by filling in the spaces.

27	sta	stb	stc	std	ste	stf
28	abt	bct	cdt	det	eft	fgt
29	aoa	bob	coc	dod	eoe	fof
30	ssh	ssi	ssj	ssk	ssl	ssm
31	34a	45b	56c	67d	78e	89f
32	r3	s4	t5	u6	v7	w8

Write the following in the order in which you would find them in the dictionary.

slippers	shoes	socks	stockings
sweater	shirt	sandals	shorts

33 (1) sandals
34 (2) shirt
35 (3) shoes
36 (4) shorts
37 (5) slippers
38 (6) socks
39 (7) stockings
40 (8) sweater

41–47 Underline any of the following words which begin and end with the same letter.

alive	fluff	bread	cocoa	dread	comic
dolls	treat	Swiss	sweet	madam	evade

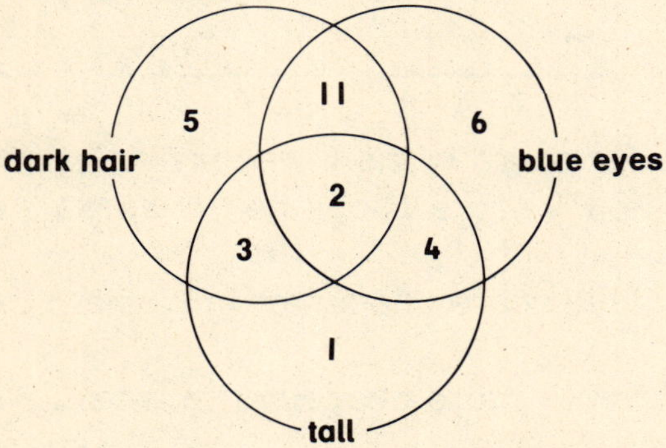

Here is a diagram we made in our class. It shows those who have dark hair, those who have blue eyes and those who are tall.

48 How many children are there in the class? 32
49 How many have blue eyes and are tall? 6
50 How many have dark hair and are tall? 5
51 How many haven't dark hair? 11
52 How many are not blue-eyed? 9
53 How many have dark hair and blue eyes? 13
54 How many are not tall? 22

a b c d e f g h i j k l m n o p q r s t u v w x y z

55 If my birthday is on the day which starts with the 6th letter of the alphabet it is on Friday

56 If **i** and **k** are next to each other, write **n**. If not, write the letter which comes after **l**. m

57 If the 9th letter is a vowel write **v** unless it comes after **h** in the alphabet in which case write **a**. a

58 If **break** contains the 5th letter of the alphabet, write **b** unless **mend** contains the 4th letter in which case write **m**. m

59 Which is the 3rd letter after the 10th? m

Underline the word which contains the same letter three times.

60 treat street terrier purser

The following are times of trains between Middlemarsh and Littlewell. Fill in the missing figures in the timetable.

		Train leaves Middlemarsh	Journey lasts	Train arrives at Littlewell
61	Train 1	9.40 a.m.	32 minutes	10.12 a.m.
62	Train 2	10.20 a.m.	30 minutes	10.50 a.m.
63	Train 3	11.15 a.m.	35 minutes	11.50 a.m.
64	Train 4	12.05 p.m.	33 minutes	12.38 p.m.

65 Which is the fastest train? 2

66 Which is the slowest train? 3

At Christmas all the presents round the Christmas tree lost their labels. There was a jigsaw, a record, a book, a pipe, a pack of cards and a crash helmet. These had to be shared among Grandad who liked smoking, Dad who was keen on indoor games, Mum who liked reading, Jenny who liked music, John who had a new motor bike and Michael who liked puzzles.

67 I would give the jigsaw to Michael

68 I would give the record to Jenny

69 I would give the book to Mum

70 I would give the pipe to Grandad

71 I would give the pack of cards to Dad

72 I would give the crash helmet to John

Write the answers to the following muddled questions.

73 is first which the month? January

74 is boy opposite the what of? girl

75 young is what a dog? puppy

76 many dog how has a legs? four

77 letter is arrive the of what fourth? i

One sum on the right has a different answer from the one on the left. Underline it.

78	**(8 × 2)**	(4 × 4 × 1)	(5 × 3) + 1	(16 + 1) × 1
79	**(4 × 3)**	(24 ÷ 8) − 1	(11 + 1) × 1	(5 × 2) + 2
80	**(3 × 7)**	(40 ÷ 2) + 1	(2 × 11 × 1)	(4 × 5) + 1
81	**(20 + 10)**	(6 × 5 × 1)	(4 × 7) − 2	(3 × 10 × 1)
82	**(5 × 5)**	(3 × 8) + 1	(2 × 11) + 3	(9 × 3) − 1

Here is some information about the weather in Kenya.

Month	Average day temperature	Average hours of sunshine	Average monthly rainfall
April	30°C	7	30 cm
May	28°C	$6\frac{1}{2}$	50 cm
June	27°C	7	18 cm
July	26°C	7	14 cm
August	26°C	$8\frac{1}{2}$	11 cm

83 The hottest of these months is (April, May, June, July, August)

84 In which month is there the most sunshine? (April, May, June, July, August)

85 The most rain comes in (April, May, June, July, August)

86 The biggest difference in rainfall from one month to the next is between (April, May, June, July, August)

87 The least difference is between (April, May, June, July, August)

88 Between which two months is there the biggest drop in day temperatures? (April, May, June, July, August)

89 Which two months have the same day temperatures? (April, May, June, July, August)

Can you do these sums in your head?

90 34 × 50 1700 91 36 × 50 1800 92 52 × 50 2600

Christine's birthday is on 23rd December.
Caroline's birthday is 8 days after Christine's and Charles' is 5 days before Caroline's.

93 When is Caroline's birthday? 31st December
94 When is Charles' birthday? 26th December

Fill in the missing figures.

95–96
```
  2467
+ 1584
  4051
```

97
```
  35
×  5
 175
```

98
```
   157
3 )471
```

99–100
```
  5566
- 3624
  1942
```

Paper 11

Two drawings on each line are the same. Underline them.

1–2

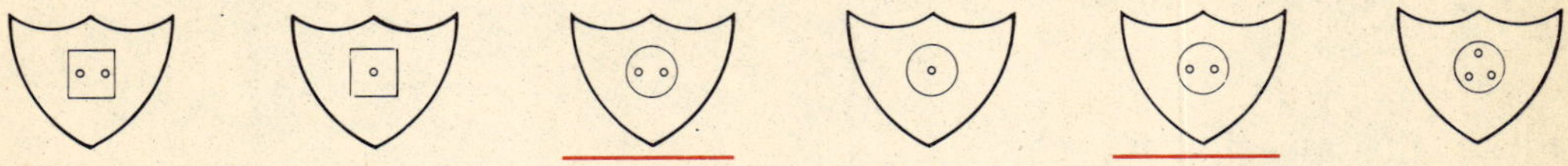

3–4

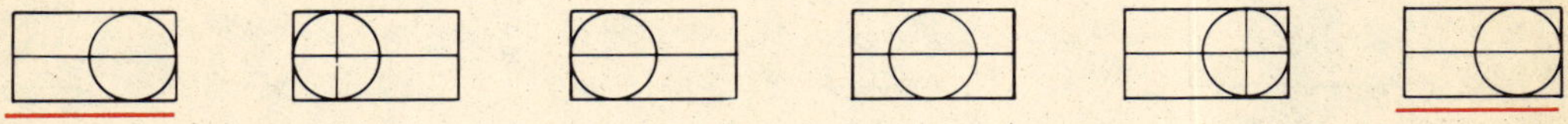

5–6

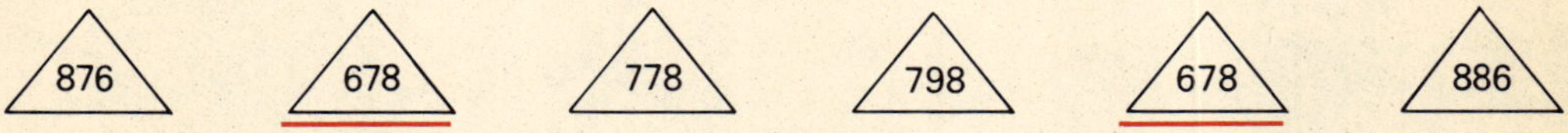

Underline the correct answer in brackets.

7 75 is to 57 as **xz** is to (**xz**, **xx**, **zx**, **zz**)

8 **rs** is to **sr** as **oq** is to (**qo**, **qq**, **oo**, **oq**)

9 Go is to come as (buy, bring, back) is to (send, seek, sell)

10 1p is to £1 as (day, year, month) is to (year, century, decade)

11 Find is to lose as (easy, earth, ebb) is to (sun, flow, world)

12 Dark is to night as (evening, light, day) is to (day, night, winter)

Below are four words and underneath are four sets of figures. They are not beneath the right words. Can you find out where they should be and work out the code?

bun	sun	bee	sat
155	768	743	143

When you have done that write these words in the code.

13 bat 168 ....

14 sat 768 ....

15 tan 863 ....

What are these words?

16 343 nun ....

17 147 bus ....

18 511 ebb ....

Underline any of the following words which forms a word when spelled backwards.

19	must	moor	male	mist	mark
20	wink	went	want	wake	wolf
21	trap	mews	mill	monk	mast
22	pads	pews	peas	seed	swap
23	emit	tune	amid	exit	tint
24	rook	pool	roof	romp	root

In each of the following lines there are six words. One of these words describes four of the other words. Underline this word and draw a ring round the word which is different from the others.

25–26	autumn	season	spring	winter	March	summer
27–28	grocer	tradesman	butcher	baker	milkman	boy
29–30	chair	bed	furniture	stool	cloth	table
31–32	hair	ankle	wrist	elbow	knee	joint
33–34	potato	orange	carrot	vegetable	onion	cabbage
35–36	aunt	brother	uncle	friend	sister	relation

Write the next word in each line.

37	tint	stint	trap	strap	tale	stale
38	gate	grate	pick	prick	tick	trick
39	same	lame	song	long	sack	lack
40	call	hall	cook	hook	come	home
41	pint	print	bake	brake	cook	crook
42	pant	paint	host	hoist	gong	going

These boys wonder how many points they scored in their last test. Do you know? If so, fill in the chart.

The scores of Tom and Gavin were formed from the same figures (8 and 5) but they did not have the same marks. Gavin had fewer marks than any of the boys. Nicholas had two marks more than Gavin but five fewer than Chris. Michael had ten marks fewer than Tom but two more than Ian.

43	Michael	75
44	Tom	85
45	Ian	73
46	Chris	65
47	Gavin	58
48	Nicholas	60

In each of the following lines underline two words which have similar meanings,

49–50	coward	weak	courage	bravery	tough	remedy
51–52	face	glance	prevent	permit	look	confess
53–54	traffic	lights	halt	car	road	stop

When the words on each line have been re-arranged to make sense, underline the one which would be the middle word of the sentence.

55 Light hands make many work

56 The crossed lady the road

57 Three and four make one

58 Christmas Day in December is

59 Picture can a paint I

60 Butter together go and bread

Philip was born in 1970. Annabel is 4 years older than Philip and Cathy is 4 years older than Annabel. In 1975 their ages were:

61 Philip ....5....

62 Annabel ....9....

63 Cathy ....13....

64 Which day of the week has seven letters in its name?

....Tuesday....

Underline the word which has the same meaning as the word at the top.

65	**abbreviate**	66	**adjacent**	67	**pursue**
	renounce		apart		follow
	shorten		opposite		hurt
	yield		near		quarrel

Can you find out what these jumbled words are?

68–74 Spend as **yanm** ....many.... days as you can on the Norfolk Broads; you will find enough **yabute** ....beauty...., interest, history, peace and **nuf** ....fun.... to keep you happy for as long as you care to **yast** ....stay..... The Broads are extremely **ruloapp** ....popular.... but **htey** ....they.... are quite big enough to give all visitors as much **capes** ....space.... and freedom as they want.

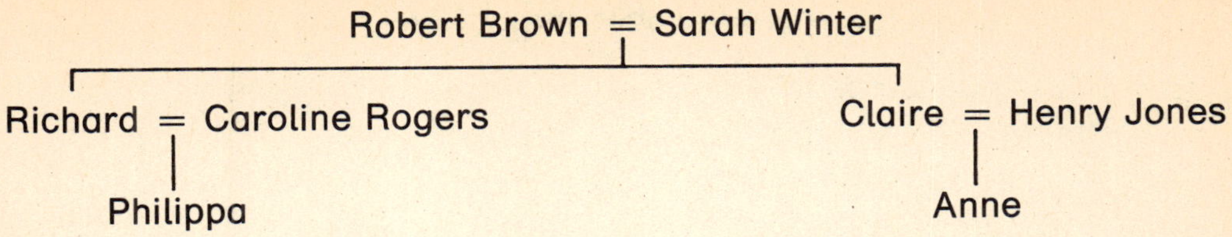

75 Philippa's surname is (Richard, Brown, Jones, Winter, Rogers)
76 Anne's surname is (Richard, Brown, Jones, Winter, Rogers)
77 Philippa is Anne's (sister, aunt, cousin, mother, friend)
78 What relation is Philippa to Sarah? (Cousin, mother, grandmother, grand-daughter, aunt)
79 Robert is Claire's (brother, father, uncle, grandfather)
80 Sarah is Richard's (mother, aunt, grandmother, sister)
81 What relation is Claire to Philippa? (Mother, aunt, grandmother, sister)
82 Who has the initials that are C.B.? (Sarah, Caroline, Claire, Anne)

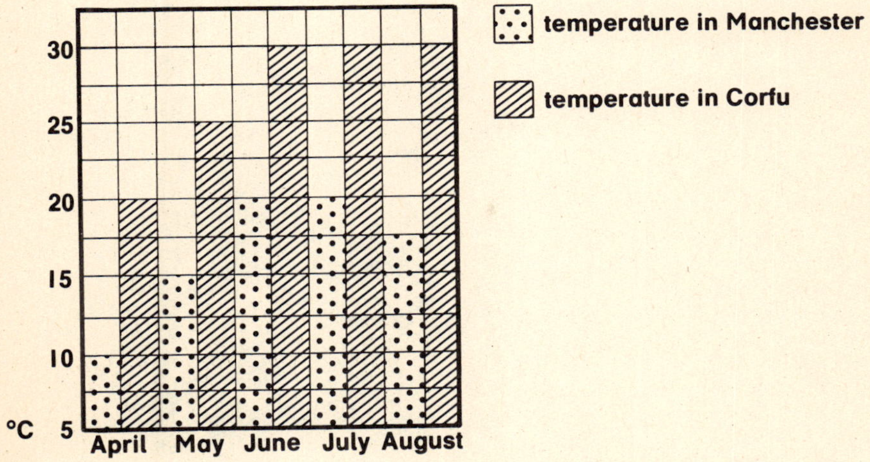

83–85 In which three months was the temperature highest in Corfu? (April, May, June, July, August)
86 In which month did Manchester have the coolest weather? (April, May, June, July, August)
87 What was the difference in temperature between the two places in May? 10°C
88 In which month was there the most difference in temperature between the two places? (April, May, June, July, August)
89 In Corfu how much higher was the temperature in July than in April? 10°C

If I heard the following remarks where might I be?

90	"Fifth floor, please."	In a lift
91	"Single to Paddington, please."	At a station
92	"Is my prescription ready?"	In a chemist's shop
93	"Next stop, please."	In a bus
94	"Is that 1234567?"	Making a telephone call
95	"Forty thirty."	At a tennis match

96 10% of £2·40 = 24p

97 10% of £4·10 = 41p

98 10% of £1·70 = 17p

99 10% of £6·90 = 69p

100 10% of £3·20 = 32p

Paper 12

In each line one drawing is different from the others. Underline the drawing.

1 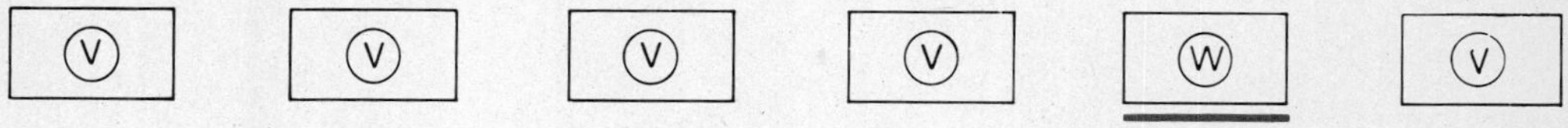

2 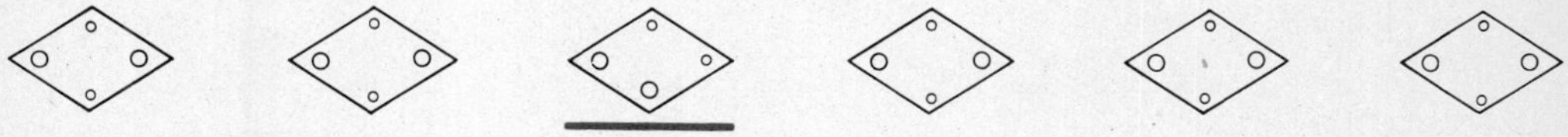

3 

4 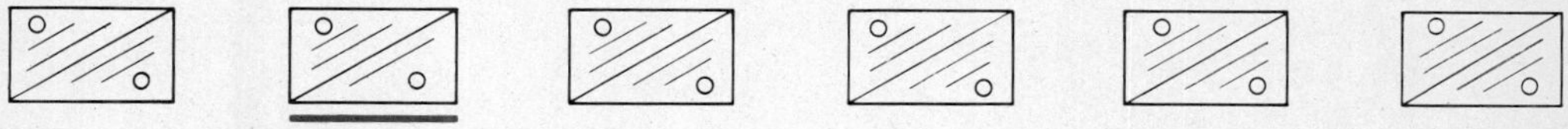

5 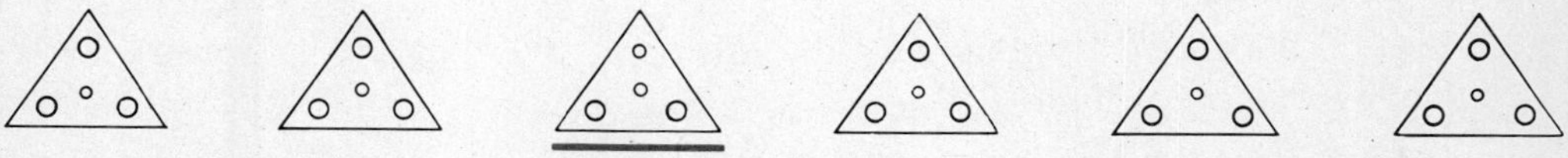

6 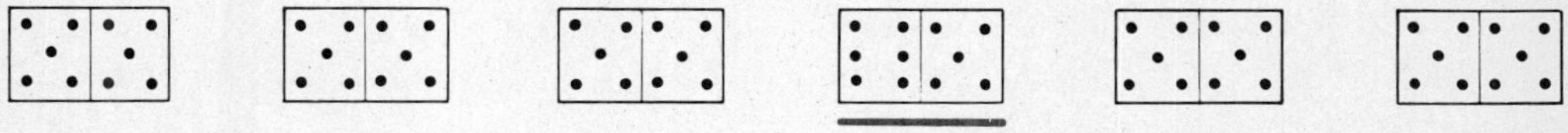

Underline a word in each pair of brackets to make sense of the sentence.

7–8 Black is to white as (snow, rain, cold) is to (hot, sun, warm)

9–10 Cat is to animal as (robin, dog, cow) is to (air, bird, fish)

11–12 Puppy is to dog as (kitten, calf, lamb) is to (lion, pig, cow)

Underline the answers that are correct.

13 $10 \times 0 = 10$

14 $2 \times \frac{1}{3} = \frac{2}{6}$

15 $20\% = \frac{1}{5}$

16 $0{\cdot}1 + 0{\cdot}1 = 1{\cdot}1$

17 50 cm = $\frac{1}{2}$ metre

18 $45 \div 5 = 9$

19 $7 \times 8 = 56$

20 $30\% = \frac{30}{100}$

21 $140 = \frac{1}{2} \times 280$

22 5p × 20 = £1

23 365 days = 1 leap year

24 October has 30 days

Below is a street plan of Endmarsh. My house is marked by a cross. Follow me as I go for a walk and, on the map, write the names of the streets and mark the buildings.

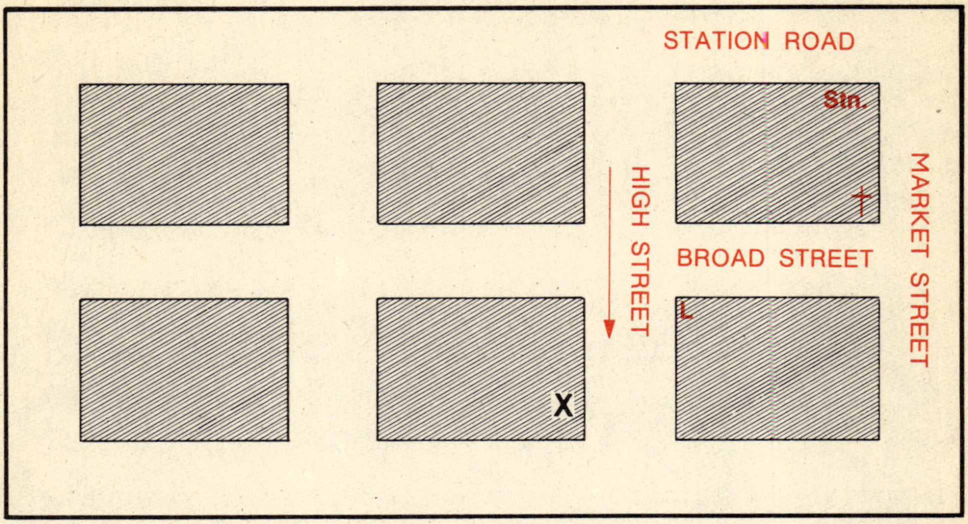

25 I come out of my house, turn left, and walk up High Street.
Mark **High Street** on the map.

26 I take the first turning on the right, and go along Broad Street.
Mark **Broad Street** on the map.

27 As I turn into Broad Street, I pass the Library on the right-hand corner of the High Street.
Mark the Library **L**.

28 I take the next turning on the left and go along Market Street.
Mark **Market Street** on the map.

29 At the left-hand corner of Broad Street is St. John's Church.
Mark the church †.

30 I then take the first turning on the left and walk along Station Road.
Mark **Station Road** on the map.

31 At the corner of Market Street and Station Road is the station.
Write **Stn.** where the station is.

32 I then take the first turning on my left and walk straight home.
Mark with an arrow.

33–34 Put a ring round the longest of these words and cross out the shortest.

cauliflower   rhododendron   chrysanthemum
~~aluminium~~   strawberry

34 a b c d e f g h i j k l m n o p q r s t u v w x y z

35 If my brother's name begins with the 15th letter of the alphabet is his name Peter, Oliver, Richard or Neil? Oliver

36 If I came top in the subject whose 1st letter is the 2nd letter after the 6th is it French, geography, history or nature study? history

37 What word would be left if all the letters which come before the 6th letter of the alphabet were crossed out from the word **bluebell**?

lull

Anthony, Shaun and Charles wore blue jeans.
Shaun, Charles and David wore navy sweaters.
David, Steven and Nicky wore red shorts.
Steven, Anthony and Nicky wore grey jumpers.

38 Who wore blue jeans and a grey jumper? Anthony

39 Who wore red shorts and a navy sweater? David

40–41 Who wore blue jeans and a navy sweater? Shaun and Charles

42–43 Who wore red shorts and a grey jumper? Steven and Nicky

One item in each line does not fit in with the others. Underline it.

44	10th	6th	8th	2nd	11
45	jumper	cardigan	skirt	pullover	sweater
46	river	hill	peak	mount	hillock
47	unkind	generous	nasty	unpleasant	cruel
48	ant	bee	fly	beetle	fir
49	coffee	sugar	tea	cocoa	milk

Underline any words which cannot be formed from the letters of the word on the left.

50	**terrace**	cart	rate	trace	erase	crate
51	**distant**	stead	stand	stain	ants	dint
52	**painter**	trip	rain	tramp	nape	print
53	**general**	large	near	rage	gear	ages
54	**detains**	stand	ends	stain	near	neat
55	**spanner**	pear	spend	spar	pans	rasp
56	**carpets**	space	star	spent	carts	traces

57 Janice, who is 10, is a year older than Paul who is 2 years younger than I am. How old am I? 11

58 My sister is 1·50 m tall. She is 3 cm taller than Mandy who is 1 cm shorter than Rosemary. How tall is Rosemary? 1·48 m

Mr. X and Mr. Y had to travel to a meeting. Mr. X went by train and the journey lasted 50 minutes. Mr. Y travelled by bus and his journey took $\frac{3}{4}$ hour. If they both left at 11.10 a.m.,

59 what time did Mr. X arrive? 12 noon

60 what time did Mr. Y arrive? 11.55 a.m.

Here is a story in which some of the words are jumbled. Write the jumbled words, which are in heavy type, correctly at the end of the line.

61 Miss Thomas was leaving at the end of the **remt**. term
62 The children were very **tpsue** as they were very upset
63 fond of her. They wanted to buy her a **teeprsn** present
64 but they couldn't make up their **nidsm** what to minds
65 get. In the end **yeht** decided to give her a book they
66 about **dribs** and a birds
67 brightly coloured **arscf**. Miss Thomas told scarf
68 them she was delighted with the **tgfis**. gifts

Complete each sentence by underlining the correct word in brackets.

69 Twelve is eight (over, more, less, than) than twenty.
70 It gets dark (earlier, later, never, sometimes) in the winter.
71 Babies are not as (round, square, tall, short) as their mothers.
72 Guy Fawkes night is in (the summer, the spring, November, May).
73 There are (more, fewer) days in February than in March.
74 The traffic lights are red, amber and (yellow, green, blue, red)
75 A clock has two (minutes, hours, hands, figures)

a 4 3 1 2 1 c a 3 4 e b 1 c 2 5 1

76 How many letters appear twice? 2
77 What is the sum of the odd numbers? 15
78 What is the sum of the even numbers? 12
79 Cross out any numbers which are between two letters.
80 Cross out a letter between two numbers.
81 Which is the 7th number? Underline it.
82 Put a ring round the 5th letter.

	Gerona	Alicante	Almeria	Malaga
Luton	2 hr 5 min	2 hr 25 min	2 hr 25 min	2 hr 45 min
Gatwick	2 hr	2 hr 20 min	——	2 hr 40 min
Heathrow	——	2 hr 35 min	2 hr 20 min	2 hr 45 min
Manchester	2 hr 25 min	2 hr 40 min	——	3 hr 15 min

83–84 On this chart which two airports have no flight to Almeria? (Luton, Gatwick, Heathrow, Manchester)

85 Which airport has no flight to Gerona? (Luton, Gatwick, Heathrow, Manchester)

86 How much longer does it take to fly to Malaga from Manchester than from Gatwick? 35 minutes

87 How much quicker is it to fly to Alicante from Gatwick than from Heathrow? 15 minutes

88–93 Can you fill in the missing words? They are all colours.

Cobalt and umber and ultramarine,
Ivory b lack and emerald g reen –
What shall I paint to give pleasure to you?
Paint for me somebody utterly new
I have painted you tigers in cri mson and w hite
The colours were good and you painted all right.
I have painted the cook and a camel in b lue
And a panther in pur ple. You painted them true.

At the end of each number (where there is space) write a figure so that:
the numbers on the top line can all be divided by 3
the numbers on the 2nd line can both be divided by 4
the numbers on the 3rd line can both be divided by 5

94–96	224 1	224 4	224 7
97–98	198 4	198 8	
99–100	176 0	176 5	

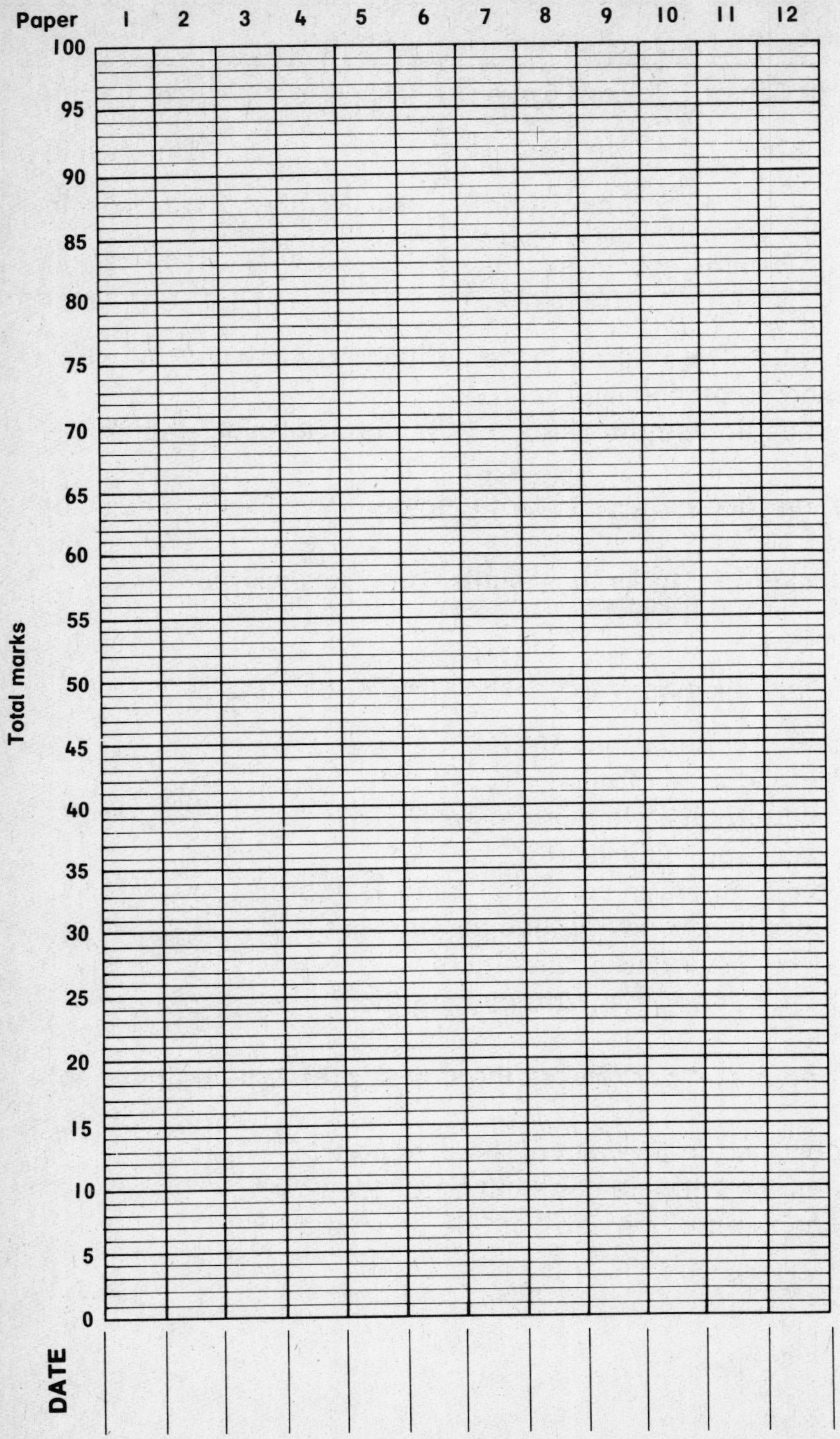
Paper
1 2 3 4 5 6 7 8 9 10 11 12
100 95 90 85 80 75 70 65 60 55 50 45 40 35 30 25 20 15 10 5 0
Total marks
DATE